Home-Baked Gifts
with Love

Home-Baked Gifts
with Love

Over 50 delicious recipes to
bake and give

CICO BOOKS

LONDON NEW YORK

www.cicobooks.com

Published in 2012 by CICO Books
An imprint of Ryland Peters & Small Ltd
20–21 Jockey's Fields, London WC1R 4BW
519 Broadway, 5th Floor, New York, NY 10012

www.cicobooks.com

10 9 8 7 6 5 4 3 2

Text © Susannah Blake, Chloe Coker, Linda Collister,
Kay Fairfax, Liz Franklin, Gloria Nicol, Annie Rigg,
Laura Tabor, Nicki Trench, Catherine Woram
Design and photography © CICO Books 2012

A CIP catalog record for this book is available from the
Library of Congress and the British Library.

ISBN: 978 1 908170 33 0

Printed in China

For digital editions, visit
www.cicobooks.com/apps.php

Editor: Jan Cutler
Designer: Louise Leffler

Note: Uncooked or partially cooked eggs
should not be served to the very young, the
very old, those with compromised immune
systems, or to pregnant women.

Contents

Introduction

Give a home-baked gift to someone and you will make them feel truly special. In this wonderful collection of over 50 recipes, you will find a delicious range of cakes and bakes, tasty cookies and gingerbread, chocolates and candy, and even preserves, chutneys, and oils. All are designed to be be made, gift-wrapped, and given with love.

You will find home-baked gifts for all occasions. For that special someone in your life there are romantic gifts, such as Raspberry Loveheart Cakes, Valentine's Cookies, and delicious chocolates. At Christmas-time give the gift of mini muffins, starry Christmas cupcakes, and Christmas Tree cakes. Add that special something to someone's Halloween party by bringing along the Jack-o-lanterns or Witches' Cats and Hats Gingerbread. For those special days, there are Wedding and Christening cupcakes, and you can even home-bake your own gift tags.

Many of the finished treats are beautifully decorated and all the techniques you need are carefully explained. To give your home-baked present that perfect finishing touch, there are some inventive gift-wrapping ideas at the end of the book.

Impress your friends and loved ones and enjoy the making and giving of these wonderful gifts.

CHAPTER 1

Cakes *and* Bakes

Make someone feel truly special by giving them a gift of delicious homemade cakes or pastries. In this chapter you'll find some gorgeous ideas such as cute and easy cupcakes, addictive mini muffins, and colorful meringues. For the one you love, you'll find a range of love heart cakes, and there are wonderful baked gifts for christenings, weddings, Halloween, and Christmas. Enjoy making and giving these easy recipes with impressive results.

Cider fruit squares

If you want all the fragrances and flavors of a Christmas cake without the work, this melt-and-mix cake is a great alternative. It contains dried fruit and spices, but it is low in fat and made without eggs. It can be served with just a dusting of confectioners'(icing) sugar.

1 In a pan large enough to hold all the ingredients, put the butter, sugar, both the raisins, chopped apricots, cider, apple pie spice, ground ginger, and ¾ cup/175ml water. Bring to a boil, stirring frequently, then reduce the heat and simmer gently for 2 minutes.

2 Remove the pan from the heat and let cool. Meanwhile, preheat the oven to 350°F/180°C/ Gas 4, and grease and baseline a 10 x 8in/25 x 20cm baking pan (tin) with baking parchment.

3 Sift the flour, baking powder, and salt into the pan, adding any fine pieces of bran remaining in the sieve. Mix with a wooden spoon until thoroughly combined.

4 Pour the mixture into the prepared baking pan, and spread evenly. Bake in the preheated oven for 25 minutes, or until it is a rich golden brown and firm to the touch.

5 Remove from the oven, and set on a wire rack to cool completely. The cake tastes best if covered tightly and left overnight before cutting. Cut into 24 squares and dust with confectioners' sugar. Store in an airtight container and eat within one week.

½ stick/50g unsalted butter, plus exra for greasing

1 cup (firmly packed)/200g brown (muscovado) sugar

⅔ cup/100g raisins

⅔ cup/100g golden raisins (sultanas)

⅓ cup/50g roughly chopped ready-to-eat dried apricots

¾ cup/175ml apple cider

1 tsp apple pie (mixed) spice

1 tsp ground ginger

2 cups/225g fine whole-wheat (wholemeal) flour, sifted to remove the bran

2 tsp baking powder

a good pinch of salt

confectioners' (icing) sugar, to dust

Makes 24

Caramel surprise

Buried in the center of each of these brownie squares is a chocolate-covered caramel, but it could just as well be a peanut butter candy or even a marshmallow, if you prefer.

1 Preheat the oven to 325°F/160°C/Gas 3, and grease and line a 9in/23cm square baking pan (tin) with greased baking parchment. Put the chocolate and butter into a heatproof bowl set over a pan of gently simmering water, making sure the bowl doesn't touch the water. Melt, stirring occasionally until smooth and thoroughly combined. Let cool slightly.

2 Add both the sugars and mix well. Add the eggs one at a time, beating well after each addition. Stir in the vanilla extract. Sift the flour and salt into the bowl, and stir until smooth.

3 Pour the mixture into the prepared baking pan and spread level. Visualize how you will be cutting the baked brownies into 25 squares—in rows and columns of five—then push the chocolate-covered caramels into the center of what will be each baked brownie square. Bake in the center of the oven for 20–25 minutes, or until the brownies are just baked.

4 Remove from the oven and let cool completely in the pan. Turn out, and cut carefully into 25 squares so that there is a caramel in the center of each square.

5 If you like, cut gold foil into squares large enough to fit around the brownies, then gift-wrap each one neatly. Cut short lengths of ribbon and tie around the gold packages.

1½ sticks/150g butter, diced, plus extra for greasing

8oz/225g bittersweet (plain) chocolate, coarsely chopped

generous ½ cup/125g superfine (caster) sugar

generous ½ cup /125g brown (muscovado) sugar

4 eggs, lightly beaten

1 tsp vanilla extract

generous 1 cup/125g all-purpose (plain) flour

a pinch of salt

25 individual chocolate-covered caramels

gold foil and ribbon, to gift-wrap (optional)

Makes 25 squares

Love hearts

The perfect Valentine's Day gift. Make the white chocolate hearts in advance and refrigerate until needed. Look for heart-shaped sugar sprinkles in bakeware stores or from online suppliers.

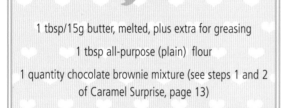

1 tbsp/15g butter, melted, plus extra for greasing

1 tbsp all-purpose (plain) flour

1 quantity chocolate brownie mixture (see steps 1 and 2 of Caramel Surprise, page 13)

For the chocolate ganache

5oz/150g bittersweet (dark) chocolate, finely chopped

²⁄₃ cup/150ml heavy (double) cream

1 tbsp brown (muscovado) sugar

a pinch of salt

To decorate

5oz/150g white chocolate, coarsely chopped

3–4 tbsp apricot or raspberry jam, warmed and sieved

red liquid food coloring

red or pink edible glitter

red heart-shaped sugar sprinkles

Makes 12

1 To make the white chocolate hearts to decorate, line a baking sheet with baking parchment. Melt the white chocolate in a heatproof bowl set over a pan of gently simmering water. Pour it onto the baking sheet and spread evenly to ¹⁄₁₆in/2mm thick. Leave in a cool place to set completely. Preheat the oven to 325°F/160°C/Gas 3.

2 Lightly brush 12 x 4in/10cm heart-shaped pans with the melted butter, and line the bases with greased baking parchment. Dust each with the flour and tip out the excess. Divide the chocolate brownie mixture among the pans. Arrange on a baking sheet and bake for 12–15 minutes. Remove from the oven and let cool in the pans for 10 minutes, then turn out onto a wire rack to cool.

3 To make the ganache, tip the chocolate into a small, heatproof bowl. Gently heat the cream and sugar in a small pan until the sugar has dissolved and the cream is just boiling. Add the salt. Pour the mixture over the chocolate and leave to melt. Stir until smooth, then cool. Brush the jam over the tops of the brownies. Leave for 5 minutes.

4 Put some red food coloring onto a saucer. Dip a clean toothbrush into it, then flick the bristles over half the white chocolate to make flecks. Sprinkle edible glitter over the other half and leave to dry. Stamp out hearts using small cutters. Spread the ganache over the brownies, and decorate with the white hearts and sprinkles.

Candied clementine with pistachios

Prepare the crystallized clementine peel at least 6 hours before you plan to serve these cakes so that they have time to dry out.

2 clementines

butter, for greasing

3 eggs

¾ cup/150g superfine (caster) sugar

1⅓ cups/150g all-purpose (plain) flour, plus extra for dusting

2 tsp baking powder

a pinch of salt

½ cup/75g ground almonds

⅓ cup/50g unsalted, shelled pistachios, finely chopped

To decorate

3 clementines

½ cup/100g superfine (caster) sugar

1 cup/125g confectioners' (icing) sugar

⅓ cup/50g unsalted, shelled pistachios, chopped

edible gold leaf (optional)

Makes 12

1 To make the crystallized peel decoration, pare the peel from the 3 clementines using a vegetable peeler, and cut into shreds. (Set the clementines aside.) Mix the shreds and sugar on a baking sheet and leave, uncovered, for 6 hours.

2 Put the 2 (unpeeled) clementines in a pan. Cover with water, bring to a boil, and simmer gently for 1 hour, or until tender. Drain and let cool. Preheat the oven to 350°F/180°C/Gas 4. Grease 12 muffin cups and lightly dust with flour, then tip out the excess.

3 Quarter the cooked clementines and remove any seeds. Purée the fruit and peel in a food processor until nearly smooth. Whisk the eggs and sugar in a large bowl until pale and thick. Sift together the flour, baking powder, and salt, then fold into the egg mixture. Fold in the almonds, pistachios, and puréed clementines. Pour into 12–14 muffin cups to fill. Bake for 15 minutes, or until well risen and a toothpick (cocktail stick) inserted into the center comes out clean.

4 Cool in the pan for 5 minutes. Run a knife around the cakes, and tip onto a wire rack to cool completely. To decorate, squeeze the juice from the reserved clementines. Sift the confectioners' sugar into a bowl, and add enough juice to make a thin icing. Spoon over each cake. Let set. Add the peel, pistachios, and gold leaf, if using.

Gingerbread mini muffins

These delightful little cakes have all the moistness of a slice of gingerbread but look very dainty made as muffins and decorated with icing. Try to buy foil cake cases, or use prettily printed ones instead.

1 Preheat the oven to 350°F/180°C/Gas 4. Line three 12-cup mini muffin pans with paper cases (or put double paper cases onto a baking sheet). Put the butter, molasses, honey, sugar, and milk in a pan over low heat, and melt gently. Remove from the heat and let cool for a couple of minutes.

2 Meanwhile, sift the flour, baking soda, ground ginger, cinnamon, and salt into a large bowl. Pour in the cooled, melted mixture, then the egg. Mix thoroughly with a wooden spoon, then mix in the stem ginger.

3 Spoon the mixture into the cases. Bake in the preheated oven for 15 minutes, or until firm to the touch.

4 Transfer to a wire rack to cool completely. Put the icing into a icing bag with a writing tip (nozzle), or use writing-icing pens, to pipe or write stars, dots or any other decoration onto the cakes. Store the cakes in an airtight container, and eat within three days.

1 stick/100g unsalted butter

2 tbsp molasses (treacle)

2 tbsp honey

½ cup packed/100g molasses (muscovado) sugar

½ cup/125ml milk

1½ cups/175g all-purpose (plain) flour

1 tsp baking soda (bicarbonate of soda)

1 tbsp ground ginger

1 tsp ground cinnamon

a good pinch of salt

1 extra-large (UK large) egg, beaten

2oz/50g preserved stem ginger, drained and finely chopped

To decorate

Royal Icing (page 132), or writing-icing pens

Makes about 36

Cakes *and* Bakes

19

White chocolate and lemon truffle balls

These buttery truffle balls flavored with lemon peel are a lovely treat. They can be made in advance and chilled until ready to serve.

3¹/₂oz/100g white chocolate, coarsely chopped

¹/₂ stick/50g butter

2 tbsp heavy (double) cream

³/₄ tsp grated lemon zest

4oz/115g pound (Madeira) cake, finely crumbled

To decorate

2oz/50g white chocolate, coarsely chopped

confectioners' (icing) sugar, for dusting

Makes about 14

1 Put the chocolate and butter in a heatproof bowl over a pan of gently simmering water, making sure the bowl doesn't touch the water. Leave to melt, gently stirring occasionally, then remove from the heat, add the cream and continue stirring until the mixture is smooth and creamy. Stir in the lemon zest, followed by the cake crumbs.

2 Take spoonfuls of the mixture, and use your fingers to roll them into walnut-sized balls. Put the balls into paper mini muffin or petit four cases, and chill for at least 2 hours, until firm.

3 To decorate, melt the 2oz/50g chocolate in a bowl set over a pan of gently simmering water, as before. Dip a skewer into the melted chocolate and drizzle zigzags of chocolate over the truffle balls. Chill until the chocolate has set. Dust lightly with confectioners' sugar just before serving.

Crystal cupcakes

These sparkling, crunchy crystal-topped cupcakes are fun for a tea party and make a stunning gift for girls. The rock candy can be dyed various colors to look like your favorite semiprecious gemstones.

1 To make the cupcakes, preheat the oven to 350°F/180°C/Gas 4, and line a 12-cup muffin pan with paper cases (or use mini muffin pans and line with mini paper cases). Put the butter and sugar in a bowl and whisk until creamy.

2 Slowly beat in the eggs one at a time. Continue to mix, then add the vanilla extract. Slowly fold in the flour. Divide among the paper cases. Bake for 18 minutes, or until springy and golden; for mini cupcakes bake for 8–10 minutes.

3 Cool in the pan on a wire rack for 3 minutes, then turn out and cool completely. To make the buttercream, put the butter and cream cheese into a large bowl. Sift over the confectioners' sugar and mix well until fluffy. Add the lemon juice and zest, and continue to mix until creamy and combined.

4 Put the rock sugar into separate bowls and add a small amount of different food coloring to each. Mix well with a small spoon until well tinted. Leave to dry for 30 minutes.

5 Divide the buttercream into separate bowls. Add a small amount of food coloring to each. Use a metal spatula to smooth the frosting over each cake. While the frosting is still wet, dip and turn each cupcake in the matching colored crystals to give them an even and encrusted layer of sparkling edible gemstones!

For the cupcakes

2½ sticks/300g butter, softened

1½ cups/300g superfine (caster) sugar

6 eggs

2 tsp vanilla extract

2¾ cups/300g self-rising (self-raising) flour, sifted

For the buttercream

7 tbsp/100g butter, softened

scant ½ cup/100g cream cheese

2¾ cups/300g confectioners' (icing) sugar

1½ tsp lemon juice

grated zest of 1 lemon

To decorate

rock sugar crystals

food coloring in assorted gem colors

Makes 12 large cupcakes

Butterfly cupcakes

A step up from the more traditional butterfly fairy cakes you might have made with your mom when you were little, these have painted fondant wings to make them look ready for flight!

For the buttermilk cake

1½ sticks/175g unsalted butter, softened

1 cup/200g superfine (caster) sugar

2 whole eggs and 1 egg yolk, beaten

1 tsp vanilla extract

2 cups/225g all-purpose (plain) flour

1 tsp baking powder

½ tsp baking soda (bicarbonate of soda)

½ cup/125ml buttermilk

For the meringue buttercream

1 cup/200g superfine (caster) sugar

3 egg whites

2 sticks/225g unsalted butter, softened and chopped

1 tsp vanilla extract

To decorate

colored sprinkles (hundreds and thousands)

confectioners' (icing) sugar, for dusting

9oz/250g white sugar paste

1 quantity Royal Icing (page 132)

pink, yellow, and brown food coloring paste

Makes 12

1 Preheat the oven to 350°F/180°C/Gas 4, and line 12 muffin cups with paper cases. To make the buttermilk cake, using an electric whisk, cream together the butter and sugar until light and creamy. Gradually add the beaten eggs, mixing well between each addition. Add the vanilla. Sift together the flour, baking powder, and baking soda, and add to the mixture in alternate batches with the buttermilk. Mix until smooth.

2 Divide the mixture among the paper cases, filling them two-thirds full, and bake for 20 minutes, or until well risen and a toothpick (cocktail stick) inserted into the center of the cupcakes comes out clean. Let cool in the pans for 5 minutes before transferring to a wire rack to cool completely.

3 To make the meringue buttercream, put the sugar and egg whites into a heatproof bowl set over a pan of gently simmering water. Whisk until it reaches at least 140°F/60°C on a candy (sugar) thermometer. Pour into a large bowl and whisk for 3 minutes, or until the mixture has cooled and doubled in volume; it should stand in stiff, glossy peaks. Gradually add the butter to the cooled meringue mix, beating constantly, until the buttercream is smooth. Fold in the vanilla.

4 Immediately spread the buttercream over the cupcakes. Scatter the sprinkles over the tops. Make the butterflies as overleaf and attach to the cakes.

Making sugar paste butterflies

1

1 Lightly dust a clean, dry work surface with confectioners' sugar. Roll the sugar paste out to a thickness of no more than ⅛in/3mm. Using a butterfly-shaped cutter, stamp out the desired number of shapes. (1)

2 Cut each butterfly in half through the body to create two wings, and set aside on baking parchment to dry out overnight. (2)

3 Divide the Royal Icing among three bowls. Tint (page 132) one pink and one yellow using the food coloring pastes; tint them the shade you like by very gradually adding more coloring. Leave the third bowl of icing white.

4 Pour 2–3 tbsp of the white icing into a piping bag with a fine writing tip (nozzle). Working on one wing at a time, pipe a border around the wing. "Flood" the inner half of the wing, nearest the butterfly's body, with white icing by spreading it to the inner edge with a mini spatula or a small knife.

5 Fill the other half of the wing with either pink or yellow icing, spreading to the outer edge and inward to meet the white icing. (3)

6 Using the tip of a skewer, drag the colored icing into the white to create a feathered effect. (4) Leave to dry. Repeat with the remaining half-wings.

7 Tint a small amount of the white icing brown, and use to pipe a small line down the center of each wing to create the body. (5) Leave to dry completely before attaching them in matching pairs to the cakes at an angle in the topping.

Advent cupcakes

You will need to make two batches of cupcakes so that you have 24 cupcakes to represent the Advent season. Make the sugar paste numbers two days in advance so that they have time to dry.

1 Make the fondant numbers two days before you make the cupcakes. Divide the fondant in half. Tint one piece pale blue using the food coloring paste, and leave the other piece untinted. Lightly dust a clean, dry work surface with confectioners' sugar. Roll the fondant out to a $\frac{1}{16}$in/2mm thickness. Using small square and round cutters, stamp out 24 shapes. Using small number cutters, stamp out the numbers 1 to 24 to represent the days of Advent. Lightly brush the underside of each number with a dab of cold water and stick them to the squares and rounds. Put on baking parchment and dry for two days.

2 Preheat the oven to 350°F/180°C/Gas 4. Line 24 muffin cups with paper cases. Divide the buttermilk cake mixture among the paper cases, filling them two-thirds full.

3 Bake for 20 minutes, or until well risen and a toothpick (cocktail stick) inserted into the center of the cakes comes out clean. Remove from the oven, and let cool in the pan for 5 minutes before transferring to a wire rack to cool completely.

4 Fill a piping bag fitted with a star tip (nozzle) with the meringue buttercream, and pipe generous swirls onto each cupcake. Dust with white and/or blue glitter. Let set for 30 minutes. Scatter more glitter onto a small plate. Dab a little cold water around the edges of the numbered shapes and dip them in the glitter. Push into the set topping.

18oz/500g white ready-to-roll fondant (sugar paste)

blue food coloring paste

confectioners' (icing) sugar, for dusting

2 quantities buttermilk cake mixture (see Butterfly Cupcakes, page 24)

2 quantities meringue buttercream (page 24)

edible white and/or blue glitter

Makes 24

Christmas mini muffins

Not as sweet as some muffins, these fruity cakes are good for breakfast or brunch served with some good coffee during the holidays when the house is full of people.

1¼ cups/150g all-purpose (plain) flour

1 tsp baking powder

a pinch of salt

¼ cup/50g superfine (caster) sugar

finely grated zest of ½ orange

½ cup/50g pecan pieces, coarsely chopped, plus 2 tbsp, to decorate

1½ tbsp raisins

½ cup/50g fresh or frozen cranberries (no need to thaw)

1 extra-large (UK large) egg, beaten

½ stick/50g unsalted butter, melted

⅓ cup/75ml milk

confectioners' (icing) sugar, to dust

Makes 30

1 Preheat the oven to 350°F/180°C/Gas 4. Line three 12-cup mini muffin pans with 30 foil or paper mini muffin cases (or put double paper cases onto a baking sheet). Sift the flour, baking powder, and salt into a large bowl. Stir in the sugar, orange zest, chopped pecans, and raisins.

2 Put the fresh or frozen cranberries into the bowl of a food processor, and chop roughly. Stir into the flour mixture.

3 Combine the beaten egg with the melted butter and milk, and stir into the flour mixture with a wooden spoon.

4 Spoon the mixture into the foil cases, then decorate with the extra pecans. Bake in the preheated oven for 12–15 minutes, or until barely golden and firm to the touch.

5 Turn out onto a wire rack. Serve warm, dusted with confectioners' sugar. When cold, store in an airtight container, and eat within two days.

Christmas trees

Here's a forest of sparkly, festively adorned trees topped with silver and gold stars. All they need now is a pile of gifts underneath them. Practice piping the "branches" to give you confidence.

1 Preheat the oven to 350°F/180°C/Gas 4, and line a 12-cup muffin pan with brown paper cases. Divide the buttermilk cake mixture among the paper cases, filling them two-thirds full.

2 Bake for 20 minutes, or until golden and well risen, and a toothpick (cocktail stick) inserted into the center of the cakes comes out clean. Remove from the oven, and let cool in the pan for 5 minutes before transferring to a wire rack to cool completely.

3 Put three-quarters of the meringue buttercream into a bowl, and tint it green using the food coloring paste. Leave the remainder untinted and spread some of this over the top of each cupcake.

4 Fill a large piping bag with a medium star tip (nozzle) with the green frosting and, working from the center, pipe pointed branch shapes towards the edges of the cupcake. Continue in this way, turning the cupcake as you go, until you have the base of a tree. Repeat with the next layer up, making the branches shorter. Carry on with more layers, making the branches ever shorter as you get to the top of the tree.

5 Dust with green glitter, and decorate with colored sugar balls. Top with a gold or silver star.

1 quantity buttermilk cake mixture (see Butterfly Cupcakes, page 24)

1 quantity meringue buttercream (see Butterfly Cupcakes, page 24)

green food coloring paste

edible green glitter

colored sugar balls

gold and silver sugar stars

Makes 12

Starry Christmas cupcakes

These pretty cupcakes will get you in the festive mood, and they are much lighter than traditional Christmas fruitcakes. Make the fondant stars the day before to let them firm up.

½ stick/50g unsalted butter, at room temperature

¼ cup packed/60g brown (muscovado) sugar

1 egg

grated zest of 1 orange

½ cup/60g self-rising (self-raising) flour

1 tbsp brandy

4 ready-to-eat dried figs, chopped

3 tbsp golden raisins (sultanas)

½ cup/70g candied (glacé) cherries, halved

To decorate

3½oz/100g blue ready-to-roll fondant (sugar paste)

3 cups/350g confectioners'(icing) sugar, sifted

3 egg whites

2½ tsp lemon juice

edible silver balls

edible clear glitter

Makes 12

1 Make the star decorations the day before you plan to make the cupcakes. Roll out the fondant, then use a mini star-shaped cookie cutter to cut out 12 stars. Set aside on baking parchment, and let dry overnight.

2 To make the cupcakes, preheat the oven to 350°F/180°C/Gas 4, and line a 12-cup muffin pan with foil or paper cases. Beat the butter and sugar together in a bowl until creamy, then gradually beat in the egg, followed by the orange zest. Sift the flour into the mixture and fold in, then stir in the brandy, followed by the dried fruit and candied cherries.

3 Spoon the mixture into the paper cases, and bake for 14 minutes, or until risen and golden, and a toothpick (cocktail stick) inserted in the center comes out clean. Transfer to a wire rack to cool completely.

4 To decorate, gradually beat the confectioners' sugar into 2 of the egg whites in a bowl until smooth and creamy, then beat in the lemon juice. Spoon the mixture over the cupcakes, and scatter over the silver balls. Let them firm up slightly.

5 Place the star decorations on top of the cupcakes, brush with the remaining egg white, and sprinkle with edible glitter.

Jack-o'-lanterns

These little carved pumpkin-shaped cakes each have their own spooky grin. Covered in bright orange sanding sugar, they look fun served on a plate decorated with vivdly colored sugar sprinkles.

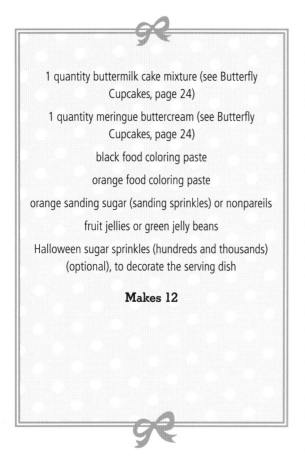

1 quantity buttermilk cake mixture (see Butterfly Cupcakes, page 24)

1 quantity meringue buttercream (see Butterfly Cupcakes, page 24)

black food coloring paste

orange food coloring paste

orange sanding sugar (sanding sprinkles) or nonpareils

fruit jellies or green jelly beans

Halloween sugar sprinkles (hundreds and thousands) (optional), to decorate the serving dish

Makes 12

1 Preheat the oven to 350°F/180°C/Gas 4. Line 12 muffin cups with orange paper cases. Divide the buttermilk cake mixture between the paper cases, filling them two-thirds full. Bake for 20 minutes, or until well risen and a toothpick (cocktail stick) inserted into the center of the cupcakes comes out clean. Let cool in the pans for 5 minutes before transferring the cakes to a wire rack to cool completely.

2 Put the meringue buttercream in a bowl. Take out 6 tbsp and put in a separate bowl. Tint this quantity black using the black food coloring. Color the remaining, large bowl of buttercream orange using the orange food coloring paste.

3 Spread the orange buttercream over the cold cupcakes, spreading evenly with an offset spatula (palette knife.) Using the blunt end of a knife or a wooden skewer, make indents in the buttercream to resemble ridges in the pumpkins. Scatter orange sanding sugar or nonpareils over the buttercream until evenly coated.

4 Fill a small piping bag with a small star-shaped tip (tube) with the black buttercream. Pipe eyes, a nose, and a mouth onto the top of the orange-frosted cakes to make Jack-o'-lantern faces. Lay the cupcakes on their sides and stick one fruit jelly into the top of each to make the stalks. If you like, scatter the serving dish with sugar sprinkles, then arrange the cupcakes on top.

Halloween cupcakes

Sweet, spicy pumpkin cupcakes topped with pretty white and bittersweet chocolate cobwebs are definitely a treat rather than a trick. The topping is best when it's still soft and gooey.

1 Preheat the oven to 350°F/180°C/Gas 4. Line a 12-cup muffin pan with colored paper cases. Put the sugar in a bowl, and break up with the back of a fork, then beat in the oil and eggs. Fold in the grated pumpkin and lemon zest. Combine the flour, baking powder, and cinnamon in a bowl, then sift into the mixture and fold in.

2 Spoon the mixture into the paper cases and bake for 18 minutes, or until risen and a toothpick (cocktail stick) inserted in the center comes out clean. Transfer to a wire rack to cool completely.

3 To decorate, put the white and bittersweet chocolates in separate heatproof bowls set over pans of gently simmering water, making sure the bowls don't touch the water. When almost melted remove from the heat and let cool for 5 minutes, then spoon the white chocolate over the cakes.

4 Cut a large square of baking parchment and fold into eighths to make a cone, then tape together. Spoon the dark chocolate into the cone, and snip off the tip so that you can pipe a thin line of chocolate. Put a dot of chocolate in the center of each cake, then pipe three concentric circles around the dot. Using a toothpick (cocktail stick), draw a line from the central dot to the outside edge of the cupcake, and repeat about eight times all the way round to create a spider's web pattern. Serve while the chocolate is still slightly soft and gooey.

½ cup packed /115g brown (muscovado) sugar

½ cup/120ml sunflower oil

2 eggs

1 cup/115g grated pumpkin or butternut squash

grated zest of 1 lemon

1 cup/115g self-rising (self-raising) flour

1 tsp baking powder

1 tsp ground cinnamon

To decorate

5oz/150g white chocolate, coarsely chopped

1oz/25g bittersweet (plain) chocolate, coarsely chopped

Makes 12

Red velvet Valentine's cupcakes

Make these mini red velvet cakes for the ones you love! Paper cupcake cases come in hundreds of colors and designs, so choose ones that will complement these adorable little Valentine's gifts.

2 cups/225g all-purpose (plain) flour

1 tsp baking soda (bicarbonate of soda)

2 heaping tbsp unsweetened cocoa powder

a pinch of salt

2 sticks/225g unsalted butter, softened

1 cup/225g superfine (caster) sugar

2 eggs, beaten

1 tsp vanilla extract

1 cup/240ml buttermilk, at room temperature

1 tsp red food coloring paste (ruby or Christmas red is best)

For the marshmallow frosting

1¼ cups/250g superfine (caster) sugar

1 tbsp water

4 egg whites

a pinch of salt

For the marzipan hearts

7oz/200g natural marzipan

red food coloring paste (ruby or Christmas red is best)
edible red glitter

Makes 18

1 Preheat the oven to 350°F/180°C/Gas 4. Line 18 muffin cups with paper cases. Sift together the flour, baking soda, cocoa powder, and salt in a large bowl.

2 Using an electric whisk, cream the butter and sugar until light. Gradually add the eggs, mixing well between each addition. Add the vanilla. With the whisk on low speed, add the dry ingredients, alternating with the buttermilk. Mix until smooth, then add enough red food coloring to make the mixture a deep red. Stir until evenly mixed.

3 Divide the mixture among the paper cases, filling them two-thirds full. Bake for 20 minutes, or until well risen and a toothpick (cocktail stick) inserted into the center comes out clean. Cool in the pans for 5 minutes, then cool on a wire rack.

4 To make the frosting, put all the ingredients in a heatproof bowl set over a pan of simmering water. Whisk slowly until the sugar has dissolved and the mixture is foamy. Continue cooking until the mixture reaches at least 140°F/60°C on a candy (sugar) thermometer. Pour the frosting into a clean bowl, and whisk on medium speed for 3 minutes, or until the frosting is stiff and glossy.

5 Immediately spoon the frosting on top of the cold cupcakes, swirling and shaping it with the back of a spoon to get a peaked effect. Make the hearts as overleaf and attach to the cakes.

Making marzipan hearts

1 Tint the marzipan red using the red food coloring paste. Then make one heart at a time. Break off a small piece of marzipan, and roll into a cylinder in the palm of your hand.

2 Gently squeeze the ends toward each other to make the top of the heart.

3 Using your fingers, squeeze the other end into a point to make the bottom of the heart.

4 Put on baking parchment, and repeat to make more hearts in assorted sizes. Dust with edible red glitter. Sit the hearts on top of the frosted cupcakes just before serving.

Wedding cupcakes

These pretty flower-topped white wedding cupcakes look gorgeous and are really simple to make. If you prefer, you can add food coloring, flowers, or ribbon to match your color scheme.

1 stick/115g unsalted butter, at room temperature

½ cup/115g superfine (caster) sugar

2 eggs

1 cup/115g self-rising (self-raising) flour

1 tsp vanilla extract or grated lemon zest

2 tbsp milk

To decorate

white lace or organza ribbon

1 egg white

1 cup/125g confectioners' (icing) sugar, sifted

½ tsp lemon juice

white edible flower decorations

Makes 12

1 Preheat the oven to 350°F/180°C/Gas 4. Line a 12-cup muffin pan with paper cases. Using an electric whisk, cream the butter and sugar together in a bowl until pale and fluffy, then beat in the eggs, one at a time, mixing well between each addition.

2 Sift the flour into the mixture and fold in. Stir in the vanilla extract or lemon zest and the milk.

3 Spoon the mixture into the paper cases and bake for 18 minutes, or until risen and golden and a toothpick (cocktail stick) inserted in the center comes out clean. Transfer to a wire rack to cool completely.

4 To decorate, carefully tie a piece of ribbon around each cupcake case. Put the egg white in a large bowl, then beat in the confectioners' sugar until thick and creamy. Beat in the lemon juice to make a thick, spoonable frosting. (If necessary, add a drizzle more lemon juice or a little more sugar to get the right consistency.)

5 Spoon the frosting onto the cupcakes, then top each one with a flower. The frosting hardens quite fast, so work quickly as soon as you've made it.

Christening cupcakes

These pretty, lemon-flavored, pastel-colored babycakes are perfect for serving at christenings or similar baby celebrations. They are just the right size for older brothers and sisters to get their little hands around, too. Choose dainty white cases or pretty patterned ones, if you can find them.

1 stick/115g unsalted butter, at room temperature

½ cup/115g superfine (caster) sugar

2 eggs

1 cup/115g self-rising (self-raising) flour

1½ tsp finely grated lemon zest

To decorate

4oz/115g cream cheese

½ cup/75g confectioners' (icing) sugar, sifted

1¼ tsp lemon juice

pink food coloring

blue food coloring

edible silver balls

Makes 24

1 Preheat the oven to 350°F/180°C/Gas 4. Line two 12-cup mini muffin pans with mini muffin or petit four cases. Using an electric whisk, cream the butter and sugar together in a bowl until pale and fluffy, then beat in the eggs, one at a time, beating well after each addition. Sift the flour into the mixture, and fold in, then stir in the lemon zest.

2 Spoon the mixture into the paper cases, then bake for 15 minutes, or until risen and golden and a toothpick (cocktail stick) inserted into the center comes out clean. Transfer to a wire rack to cool completely.

3 To decorate the cakes, beat the cream cheese briefly until soft. Gradually beat in the sugar until smooth and creamy, then stir in the lemon juice.

4 Divide the frosting between two bowls, add a few drops of food coloring to each one, and stir well to make baby pink and pastel blue. Swirl the frosting on top of the cupcakes, then sprinkle the silver balls over the top.

Raspberry love heart cakes

Bake a batch of these delightfully flirtatious cupcakes filled with a zesty lemon cream and fresh raspberries for the one you love, and they'll never have eyes for anyone but you! For that extra-special touch, buy a muffin pan with heart-shaped cups, and push your regular paper cases into the cups.

1 Preheat the oven to 350°F/180°C/Gas 4. Line a 12-cup muffin pan (heart-shaped if possible) with paper cases. Cream the butter and sugar together in a bowl until pale and fluffy, then beat in the eggs, one at a time, beating well after each addition. Sift the flour into the mixture and fold in, then stir in the lemon zest and juice.

2 Spoon the mixture into the paper cases, and bake for 18 minutes, or until risen and golden and a toothpick (cocktail stick) inserted into the center comes out clean. Transfer to a wire rack to cool completely.

3 To decorate, using a sharp, pointed knife, remove a deep round from the center of each cupcake, just over 1in/2.5cm in diameter.

4 Slice the pointed end off each piece of cored-out cupcake so that you are left with a disk. Using a mini heart-shaped cookie cutter, cut the disks into hearts.

5 Combine the crème fraîche or sour cream and lemon curd in a bowl, then fold in the raspberries. Spoon the mixture into the hollowed-out cupcakes, then top with the hearts. Dust generously with confectioners' sugar.

1 stick/115g unsalted butter, at room temperature

½ cup/115g superfine (caster) sugar

2 eggs

1 cup/115g self-rising (self-raising) flour

grated zest and juice of ½ lemon

To decorate

⅓ cup/75ml crème fraîche or sour cream

1 tbsp lemon curd

⅔ cup/70g raspberries

confectioners' (icing) sugar, for dusting

Makes 12

Meringue mountain

This is a foolproof method for making meringues that are slightly chewy in the center but still crisp on the outside. If you can, make the meringue mixture in an electric freestanding mixer, as it takes 10 minutes for it to become stiff and glossy. The cooked meringues will store for three to four days in an airtight container.

1½ cups/300g superfine (caster) sugar

5 extra-large (UK large) egg whites

pink food coloring paste

blue food coloring paste

1 tbsp unsweetened cocoa powder

edible colored balls and colored sprinkles (hundreds and thousands)

Makes 12

1 Preheat the oven to 400°F/200°C/Gas 6, and line two baking sheets with baking parchment. Tip the sugar into a small roasting pan and warm in the oven for about 7 minutes, or until hot to the touch. Reduce the heat to 110°C/225°F/Gas ¼.

2 Meanwhile, in a clean grease-free bowl, whisk the egg whites using an electric mixer until frothy. Tip all the hot sugar onto the egg whites and continue to mix on high speed for 10 minutes, or until the meringue is very stiff, white, and cold. Divide the mixture among three bowls.

3 Add tiny amounts of pink food coloring paste to one bowl, using a toothpick (cocktail stick), and very gently fold in using a large metal spoon until the color has marbled the mixture. Using two tablespoons, dollop the meringue into four even-sized mounds on the prepared baking sheets. Repeat with the blue food coloring paste.

4 Sift the cocoa into the last bowl of meringue mixture, and gently fold in until it is marbled with cocoa. Spoon onto the baking sheets as before. Sprinkle edible colored balls and sprinkles over the meringues, then bake for 1½–1¾ hours. Let cool on the baking sheets. Pile the meringues on a plate to serve.

Raspberry and lemon Napoleons

Nothing beats the experience of breaking through the crisp pastry layers of a Napoleon to reach the sweet cream and fruit layered within. These simplified individual versions of the classic French pâtisserie (also known as "millefeuille") are easy to put together, yet they look utterly sophisticated and taste divine.

butter, for greasing

9oz/250g all-butter puff pastry, thawed if frozen

flour, for dusting

5 tbsp lemon curd

1¼ cups/300ml crème fraîche or sour cream

3½ cups/400g raspberries

confectioners' (icing) sugar, to dust

Makes 8

1 Preheat the oven to 400°F/200°C/Gas 6, and lightly grease a baking sheet. Roll out the puff pastry on a lightly floured work surface to a thickness of ¼in/5mm, then trim it to a 12 x 6in/ 30 x 15cm rectangle.

2 Slice the dough into eight squares of equal size, and arrange them on the baking sheet. Bake for about 10 minutes, or until puffed up and golden. Transfer to a wire rack to cool completely.

3 Once cool, use a serrated knife to carefully cut each pastry square in half horizontally to create 16 pieces. When ready to assemble the pastries, arrange eight of the pastry rectangles on a serving platter. Fold the lemon curd into the crème fraîche or sour cream, and spread about 2 tbsp of the lemon cream on top of each one.

4 Top with raspberries and a second pastry rectangle. Dust liberally with confectioners' sugar and serve immediately.

White chocolate and raspberry tartlets

These indulgent little fresh fruit tarts look elegant and taste good, yet they are very simple to prepare, made with "all-butter" puff pastry for the best flavor. They are a lovely surprise treat to make as a gift.

10oz/300g all-butter puff pastry, thawed if frozen

flour, for dusting

4oz/115g good-quality white chocolate, coarsely chopped

2 eggs

6 tbsp/90ml heavy (double) cream

1/4 cup/50g superfine (caster) sugar

2 1/2 cups/300g fresh raspberries

confectioners' (icing) sugar, to dust

Makes 12

1 Preheat the oven to 350°F/180°C/Gas 4. Roll out the pastry on a lightly floured work surface to a thickness of 1/8in/3mm. Cut the dough into rounds using a cookie cutter that is roughly the same size as the cups of a 12-cup muffin pan. Press the pastry discs gently into the muffin cups.

2 Put the chocolate into a heatproof bowl set over a pan of gently simmering water, making sure the bowl doesn't touch the water. Melt gently, then stir the chocolate with a wooden spoon. Remove from the heat and let cool slightly.

3 Put the eggs into a large bowl and beat with a balloon whisk until smooth. Whisk in the cream and sugar. Whisk in the melted chocolate until the mixture is smooth.

4 Carefully fill the pastry shells with the white chocolate mixture using a small spoon. Bake for 15 minutes, or until the pastry is puffy and golden and the filling is risen (it will fall as the tartlets cool.) Leave the tartlets to cool in the pan, then carefully turn them out. Arrange 3 raspberries on top of each tartlet and dust lightly with confectioners' sugar. These tartlets are best eaten on the day they are made. Store refrigerated until ready to serve.

Cheese palmiers

Folded puff pastry "hearts", flavored with a mixture of cheese and mustard, are quite simple to assemble and look very professional—the perfect gift for someone who prefers a savory to something sweet.

4oz/115g Parmesan or Grana Padano cheese, finely grated

12oz/340g all-butter puff pastry, thawed if necessary

1 tbsp Dijon mustard

½ tsp mild paprika

¼ tsp cayenne pepper or ground black pepper

Makes 36

1 Line two baking sheets with baking parchment. Sprinkle a little of the grated cheese on the work surface and gently unroll the pastry or, if necessary, roll out to a rectangle about 9 x 15in/ 23 x 38cm. Spread the mustard over the pastry with a round-bladed knife. Mix the remaining cheese with the paprika and pepper, then scatter over the pastry.

2 Fold the pastry as follows, but don't fold too tightly or the pastry won't puff up in the oven—it is supposed to resemble a palm leaf. Fold each long side over towards the center, then fold each side over again so that there are four layers of pastry on each side of the center. Now, fold one folded side of pastry on top of the other to make a log shape.

3 Using a sharp knife, cut into slices about ¼in/5mm thick. Arrange the slices on the prepared baking sheets spaced well apart to allow for spreading, and leave the two halves of the "U" shape slightly open so that the pastry can puff up. Chill for 15 minutes. Meanwhile, preheat the oven to 425°F/220°C/Gas 7.

4 Bake for 8–10 minutes, or until crisp, well-puffed, and golden. Transfer to a wire rack to cool completely. Store in an airtight container and eat within one day—if necessary warm them through in a low oven before serving, to crisp up.

CHAPTER 2

Cookies *and* Gingerbread

Perhaps one of the most fun and creative aspects of making cookies for gifts is that many of them can be decorated. In this chapter you will find delightful baby shoes to celebrate a birth or christening, as well as patterned hats for Mother's Day, hanging love hearts for Valentine's Day, or just to say "I love you," and bold polka-dot presents for almost any occasion. There are also plenty of simpler, tempting and stunning cookies that you will love to make, including traditional favorites such as gingerbread men, and the delicious and chocolatey Florentines and Lebkuchen.

Mini florentines

Who can resist the combination of chocolate, crisp nuts, and chewy fruit in this traditional favorite? These mini florentines make very impressive treats when presented in a small box or wrapped in cellophane and tied with a pretty ribbon.

1 Preheat the oven to 350°F/180°C/Gas 4, and line three baking sheets with baking parchment. Put the butter, sugar, and syrup into a pan and heat gently until the butter has melted. Remove from the heat.

2 Add the flour, cherries, candied peel, and nuts to the mixture, and stir well. Spoon half-teaspoonfuls of the mixture onto the baking sheets, allowing space for the florentines to expand as they cook.

3 Bake for 8–10 minutes, or until golden brown. Allow to cool on the paper before transferring them to a wire rack to cool completely.

4 Put the chocolate in a heatproof bowl over a pan of gently simmering water, making sure the bowl doesn't touch the water. Heat gently until the chocolate has completely melted. Stir gently.

5 Spread a small amount of melted chocolate over the base of each florentine. Let set, chocolate-side up, on the wire rack. Store in an airtight container for up to one week.

½ stick/50g unsalted butter

¼ cup/50g light brown (demerara) sugar

4 tbsp corn (golden) syrup

½ cup/50g all-purpose (plain) flour

4 candied (glacé) cherries, finely chopped

⅓ cup/50g mixed candied peel, finely chopped

½ cup/50g mixed almonds and walnuts, finely chopped

6oz/175g good-quality bittersweet (plain) chocolate, coarsely chopped

Makes 14

Chocolate chip biscotti

Crisp, crunchy chocolate cookies studded with chunks of bittersweet chocolate and pecans are lovely with ice cream as well as hot drinks.

3 extra-large (UK large) eggs, at room temperature

1 cup packed/200g brown (muscovado) sugar

finely grated zest of 1 orange

1 stick/115g unsalted butter, melted

2¾ cups/325g all-purpose (plain) flour, plus extra for dusting

1 tbsp baking powder

generous ¼ cup/25g unsweetened cocoa powder

1 cup/100g pecan pieces

3½oz/100g bittersweet (plain) chocolate, coarsely chopped

Makes about 36

1 Preheat the oven to 350°F/180°C/Gas 4, and line two baking sheets with baking parchment. Put the eggs, sugar, and orange zest in a bowl and whisk with an electric mixer until very frothy. Whisk in the melted butter.

2 Sift the flour, baking powder, and cocoa into the bowl and mix with a wooden spoon. Work in the pecans and chopped chocolate.

3 When thoroughly combined, turn out the dough onto a floured work surface and divide into two equal portions. Using well floured hands, lift a portion of dough onto each prepared baking sheet and shape into a brick about 12 x 3in/ 30 x 7.5cm—they will spread in the oven. Bake for 25–30 minutes, or until just firm when pressed.

4 Remove the baking sheets from the oven (turn off the oven) and let cool completely.

5 When ready to continue, reheat the oven to 350°F/180°C/Gas 4. Using a serrated bread knife, slice the logs, while still on the baking sheets, on the diagonal about ½in/1cm thick. Put, cut-side down, on the baking sheets and return to the oven. Bake for 10 minutes, or until crisp and dry.

6 Transfer the biscotti to a wire rack to cool completely. Store in an airtight container and eat within three weeks.

Mint chocolate kisses

This is the kind of treat to put a smile on your face—it has something to do with the nostalgic combination of chocolate, peppermint, and brightly colored sprinkles.

6oz/175g bittersweet (plain) chocolate, coarsely chopped

1½ sticks/175g unsalted butter

2 eggs

generous 1 cup packed/225g brown (muscovado) sugar

2 cups/250g self-rising (self-raising) flour

¾ tsp baking powder

a pinch of salt

For the minty buttercream

¾ stick/75g unsalted butter, softened

1⅓ cups/150g confectioners' (icing) sugar, sifted

½–1 tsp peppermint extract

To decorate

7oz/200g bittersweet (plain) chocolate, chopped

colored sprinkles (hundreds and thousands)

Makes about 18

1 Put the chocolate and butter into a heatproof bowl over a pan of gently simmering water, making sure the bowl doesn't touch the water. Stir until smooth and combined. Put the eggs and sugar into a bowl, and whisk with an electric whisk until pale and light. Mix in the chocolate mixture. Sift the flour, baking powder, and salt into the bowl and stir until smooth. Bring the dough together, then cover and chill for 2 hours.

2 Preheat the oven to 350°F/180°C/Gas 4, and line two baking sheets with baking parchment. Pull off walnut-sized pieces of dough and roll into balls. Arrange on the prepared baking sheets. Bake in batches in the center of the oven for 12 minutes, or until crisp on the edges but slightly soft in the center. Let cool on the baking sheets for a few minutes before transferring to a wire rack to cool completely.

3 To make the minty buttercream, put the butter in a large bowl and beat it with an electric whisk until very soft. Gradually add the confectioners' sugar and beat until pale and smooth. Add peppermint extract to taste. Sandwich the cookies together with the buttercream.

4 To decorate, melt the chocolate in a heatproof bowl set over a pan of gently simmering water, as before. Stir, then let cool slightly. Half-dip the cookies in the chocolate, scatter with sprinkles and leave on baking parchment to set.

Swedish pepper cookies

Traditionally made for the Christmas holidays, these dark spicy cookies can be left plain or decorated with white icing—ready-made icing writing pens are perfect for this.

1⅔ cups/200g all-purpose (plain) flour, plus extra for dusting

½ tsp baking soda (bicarbonate of soda)

1 tsp ground cinnamon

1 tsp ground ginger

½ tsp ground black pepper

freshly grated zest of 1 orange

¾ cup/150g superfine (caster) sugar

1 stick/115g unsalted butter, chilled and diced

1 egg, lightly beaten

1 tbsp molasses (treacle)

Makes about 15

1 Put all the ingredients in a food processor and blend until the mixture forms a soft dough. (Alternatively, mix thoroughly using a wooden spoon or electric whisk.)

2 When thoroughly combined, shape the dough into a ball and wrap in plastic wrap (clingfilm). Chill for 1 hour, or until firm.

3 Preheat the oven to 325°F/160°C/Gas 3, and grease two baking sheets. Remove the dough from the refrigerator, unwrap, and roll out on a lightly floured work surface until about ¼in/5mm thick. Dip a star-shaped cookie cutter in flour and cut out shapes. Gather up the trimmings and re-roll, then cut out more shapes. Arrange the cookies slightly apart on the prepared baking sheets and chill for 10 minutes.

4 Bake for 10–12 minutes, or until dark golden brown and firm. Let cool for 5 minutes, then transfer to a wire rack to cool completely. Store in an airtight container and eat within one week or freeze for up to one month.

Fancy hats

These pretty hats make a perfect gift for Mother's Day or as part of a picnic hamper for a summer event. Decorate them in pastel colors with polka dots, streamers, flowers, bows, or feathers.

For the cookies

2¼ cups/250g all-purpose (plain) flour

1 cup/125g self-rising (self-raising) flour

pinch of salt

2 sticks/225g unsalted butter, at room temperature

⅔ cup/125g unrefined superfine (golden caster) sugar

1 egg yolk

1 tsp vanilla extract

To decorate

12 marshmallows (optional)

¼ quantity white Royal Icing (page 132)

confectioners' (icing) sugar, for dusting

4oz/125g each pink, purple, and white ready-to-roll fondant (sugar paste)

Makes 12

1 To make the cookies, sift the flours and salt into a large bowl, and set aside. Using an electric whisk, cream the butter and sugar in another bowl until light and fluffy. Beat in the egg yolk and vanilla extract. Add the flours and mix everything together until all the flour is incorporated, and the mixture forms a dough. Stop mixing as soon as the flour is combined, as you do not want to overwork the dough.

2 Wrap the dough in plastic wrap (clingfilm) and chill for at least 1 hour. Preheat the oven to 400°F/200°C/Gas 6, and line a baking sheet with baking parchment.

3 Roll out the cookie dough, and cut out 12 large cookies using a large round or an oval cookie cutter. The crown of each hat is made using a marshmallow or a small disc of dough; if you not using marshmallows, cut out 12 small cookies using a small cookie cutter. Put all the cookies on the baking sheet and chill for 30 minutes. Bake for 12–16 minutes, or until the cookies are golden. Transfer to a wire rack and let cool completely. To assemble and decorate the hats, see overleaf.

4 Using Royal Icing, stick the small cookies, or the marshmallows, if using, in the center or to one side of the large cookies.

5 Dust the work surface with confectioners' sugar and roll out the pink, purple, and white fondants. For hats with a polka-dot design, use the technique on page 134. Using a cutter a little larger than the one used for the large cookies, cut out three rounds or ovals from each color. Lay each round of rolled fondant over a hat and smooth it down with your fingers.

6 Decorate the hats in different ways. For ribbons with a polka-dot design, use the technique as for step 5.

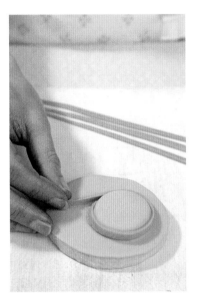 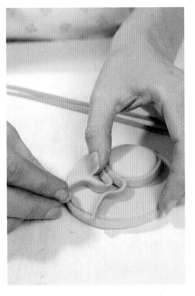 

7 Using some of the fondant trimmings, cut out a thin strip and attach it around the crown of each hat.

8 Cut out more strips in various colors and lay them along the hats as ribbons or streamers.

9 Cut out triangles into some of the "ribbons" at the ends and add a bow by following the instructions in step 3 on page 72.

10 Add flowers to some hats, using a cutter.

11 To make a feather, roll a ball of fondant between your fingers. Shape the ball into a long teardrop and then squash it flat with your thumb. Use a knife to make small cuts along the edge to look like a feather.

Polka-dot presents

These colorful cookie presents make a delightful Christmas gift, or you can change the colors to make them suitable for any other special occasion. The bows are quick and simple to make, but if you don't have time to make them, simply cover the cookies with rolled fondant and tie them with real ribbons.

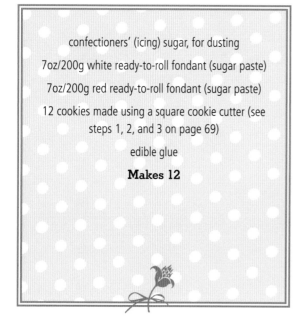

confectioners' (icing) sugar, for dusting

7oz/200g white ready-to-roll fondant (sugar paste)

7oz/200g red ready-to-roll fondant (sugar paste)

12 cookies made using a square cookie cutter (see steps 1, 2, and 3 on page 69)

edible glue

Makes 12

1 Dust the work surface with confectioners' sugar. Make some polka-dot fondant (page 134). Cut out squares of the rolled fondant the same size as the cookies.

2 Stick the fondant to the cookies using edible glue. Roll out some fondant to ⅛in/3mm thick and cut strips about ½in/1cm wide. Attach two strips to each cookie for the ribbons.

3 To make a bow, cut out a strip of red fondant about ½in/1cm wide and twice the length that you would like the bow to be. Take one end and fold it into the center, making sure that the curl stands open (you can use the end of a paintbrush or some rolled-up paper towel/kitchen paper to support it.) Fold in the other half so that the ends meet in the center. Lay the bow across another, slightly thinner and shorter, strip of rolled fondant. Fold in the ends of this strip and turn the bow over. Finally, gently squeeze the sides to shape the bow.

4 To make the ribbon tails for each cookie, cut a strip of rolled fondant ½in/1cm wide. Cut it in half and cut little triangles in the ends. Attach the strips to the center of the cookie and stick the bow on top.

Gingerbread shapes

Lightly golden and well spiced, these are richer than the usual gingerbread men, but for a deeper colour replace the light brown (demerara) sugar with dark brown (muscovado) sugar.

1 Sift the flour, ginger, baking soda, and cinnamon into a large bowl. Put the butter, sugar, and corn syrup into a pan large enough to hold all the ingredients. Set over low heat to melt very gently. Remove the pan from the heat and add all the sifted ingredients. Mix thoroughly with a wooden spoon to make a firm dough. Leave until cool enough to handle. Turn out onto a work surface and knead gently to make a neat ball, then wrap in plastic wrap (clingfilm) and chill for 20 minutes, or until firm.

2 Preheat the oven to 350°F/180°C/Gas 4, and line two baking sheets with baking parchment. Roll out the dough on a lightly floured work surface until 1/4in/5mm thick. Dip a variety of shaped cookie cutters in flour and cut out cookies. Gather up the trimmings and re-roll, then cut out more. Arrange the cookies slightly apart on the baking sheets. Bake for 8–10 minutes, or until lightly browned. If using as hanging decorations, use a toothpick (cocktail stick) to make a small hole at the top of each shape large enough to thread a ribbon through. Transfer to a wire rack to cool completely.

3 Decorate with Royal Icing or Glacé Icing using a piping bag with a writing tip (nozzle), or use a writing icing pen, to draw lines around each shape. Add silver balls while the icing is still wet. Let set. Thread with ribbons, if using for decorations. Store the shapes in an airtight container and eat within one week.

3 cups/350g all-purpose (plain) flour, plus extra for dusting

1 tbsp ground ginger

1 tsp baking soda (bicarbonate of soda)

1 tsp ground cinnamon

1½ sticks/175g unsalted butter

¾ cup packed/150g light brown (demerara) sugar

4 tbsp corn (golden) syrup

To decorate

Royal Icing (page 132), or writing icing pens

edible silver balls

ribbons (optional)

Makes 12–18

French chocolate fingers

Made with a light and sweet buttery dough, these elegant piped chocolate cookies are drizzled with bittersweet chocolate. They really do melt in the mouth, and make perfect gifts to serve with a creamy dessert or simply with coffee.

1½ sticks/175g unsalted butter,
at room temperature

¼ cup/50g superfine (caster) sugar

½ tsp vanilla extract

¼ cup/25g unsweetened cocoa powder

1¼ cups/150g all-purpose (plain) flour

½ tsp baking powder

To decorate

3oz/75g bittersweet (plain) or white chocolate,
coarsely chopped

Makes about 30

1 Preheat the oven to 350°F/180°C/Gas 4, and line two baking sheets with baking parchment. Put the butter, sugar, and vanilla extract into a bowl and beat with an electric whisk until light and fluffy. Sift in the cocoa, flour, and baking powder, and fold in until thoroughly combined.

2 Spoon the mixture into a piping bag with a fluted nozzle. Pipe the mixture onto the prepared baking sheets in fingers 4in/10cm long, spacing them well apart to allow for spreading during baking. Bake for 15 minutes, or until slightly colored around the edges.

3 Remove from the oven and let cool completely on the baking sheets—be careful, the cookies are quite fragile.

4 To decorate, melt the chocolate in a heatproof bowl over a pan of gently simmering water, making sure the bowl doesn't touch the water. Dip a fork or teaspoon into the chocolate and drizzle it over the cold cookies. Let set, then store in an airtight container and eat within five days.

Mini gingerbread men

These are so cute! You can buy all sorts of shapes and sizes of gingerbread men cutters. For this recipe, use a small cutter—you will get more cookies, and they also look great hung on the Christmas tree.

1 Preheat the oven to 375°F/190°C/Gas 5. Lightly grease three large baking sheets. Put the flour, baking soda, and ginger into a bowl, then rub in the butter until the mixture resembles breadcrumbs.

2 Stir in the sugar, and then add the syrup and egg to the mixture. Mix to form a dough, kneading lightly with your hands, if necessary.

3 Lightly flour your work surface and divide the dough in half. Roll out one half to a thickness of ¼in/5mm. Using a mini gingerbread man cutter, cut out the shapes and place them on the baking sheets. Decorate them by using currants for eyes and buttons. Repeat, using the other half of the dough mixture.

4 Bake in the oven for 10–12 minutes, or until a dark golden color. Leave the gingerbread men to cool slightly before transferring them to a wire rack to cool completely. Tie ribbon bows around the gingerbread men to decorate. Store in an airtight container and eat within one week.

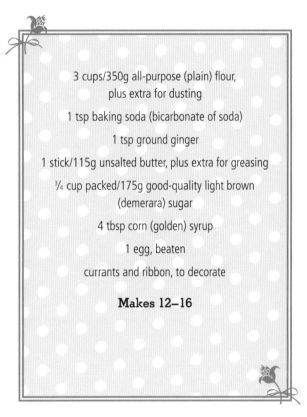

3 cups/350g all-purpose (plain) flour, plus extra for dusting

1 tsp baking soda (bicarbonate of soda)

1 tsp ground ginger

1 stick/115g unsalted butter, plus extra for greasing

¾ cup packed/175g good-quality light brown (demerara) sugar

4 tbsp corn (golden) syrup

1 egg, beaten

currants and ribbon, to decorate

Makes 12–16

Baby shoes

Present these dainty cookies to proud new parents or to celebrate baby's first birthday. Make them pretty and girly with lacy edging and little flowers, or cool and fun for little boys with buttons, stars, and polka dots.

12 cookies made using a baby shoe cookie cutter (see steps 1, 2, and 3 on page 69)

½ quantity pink or blue Royal Icing (page 132)

¼ quantity white Royal Icing (page 132)

¼ quantity yellow Royal Icing (page 132)

confectioners' (icing) sugar, for dusting

3½oz/100g white ready-to-roll fondant (sugar paste)

edible glue

Makes 12

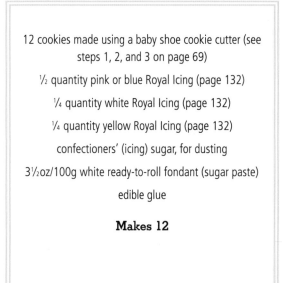

1 Using a colored Royal Icing, outline and flood a cookie using a piping bag with a fine tip (nozzle) for the outline and a large tip for the flooding, following the steps on page 134. Repeat for the other cookies using the pink or blue, and the white and yellow icings.

2 Add polka dots to some cookies while the icing is still wet, by dropping dots of white into the colored icing, following the wet-on-wet technique on page 134.

3 When the icing has dried, pipe a border around the cookies using a fine tip.

4 Dust the work surface with confectioners' sugar and roll out the white fondant. Using a small or medium flower cutter, star, heart, or circle cutter, cut out shapes for "buttons" for the shoe fasteners and attach with edible glue. Make holes in the "buttons" using a toothpick (cocktail stick).

Valentine cookies

Make these delicious heart-shaped cookies and decorate them with colorful frosting and a pretty bow. Wrap them in a cellophane bag tied with matching ribbon as a gift for Valentine's Day.

¾ stick/75g unsalted butter, plus extra for greasing

½ cup/100g superfine (caster) sugar

1 extra-large (UK large) egg

1¼ cups/150g all-purpose (plain) flour, plus extra for dusting

½ tsp baking powder

½ tsp salt

tubes of ready-to-use icing in white and red

ready-made sugar flowers

ribbon

cellophane bags (optional)

Makes 25

1 Using an electric whisk, cream the butter and sugar together in a bowl until soft, then beat in the egg. Sift in the flour, baking powder, and salt. Fold in to mix. Roll the dough into a ball, wrap in plastic wrap (cliingfilm), and chill for 1 hour.

2 Preheat the oven to 350°F/180°C/Gas 4, and grease a baking sheet. Sprinkle some flour onto the work surface, then roll the dough to about ¼in/5mm thick. Cut out heart shapes using a cookie cutter.

3 Use a drinking straw to pierce a hole at the center top of each heart cookie prior to baking. Space the cookies evenly across the baking sheet. Bake the cookies for 10–12 minutes, or until golden brown—the thinner the cookie is rolled, the shorter the baking time. Transfer the cookies to a wire rack and let cool completely.

4 Use tubes of white and red ready-to-use icing to apply tiny dots around the edge of each cookie.

5 Use a dab of icing to stick a sugar flower to the center of each heart and let dry. Cut an 8in/20cm length of ribbon for each cookie and thread through the pierced hole. Tie the ribbon in a bow, then trim the ribbon ends across diagonally with sharp scissors to prevent them from fraying. Pack in cellophane bags, if you like.

Chocolate gingerbread

Gingerbread with a difference. This is a delicious family favorite even without the frosting and with chocolate fudge frosting on top it makes a special gift. You can leave it whole as a large cake or cut into squares to be served as an after-dinner treat.

1 cup/200g dark brown (muscovado) sugar

1 stick/115g unsalted butter, plus extra for greasing

1 cup/250g corn (golden) syrup

3½ cups/400g all-purpose (plain) flour

1½ tsp baking powder

½ tsp baking soda (bicarbonate of soda)

2½ tsp ground ginger

1 egg, lightly beaten

⅔ cup/150ml whole milk

Chocolate fudge frosting

1¼ cups/150g confectioners' (icing) sugar, sifted

¼ cup/25g unsweetened cocoa powder, sifted

½ stick/50g unsalted butter, softened

scant 1 cup/100g finely chopped nuts (optional)

Makes about 16

1 Preheat the oven to 300°F/150°C/Gas 2, and grease and line a 9in/23cm cake pan (tin). Put the sugar, butter, and corn syrup into a large pan. Heat gently over low heat, stirring continuously, until the sugar has dissolved completely. Set aside to cool.

2 Sift the flour, baking powder, baking soda, and ground ginger into a bowl. Pour the cooled syrup over the dry ingredients, and add the egg and milk. Stir until smooth.

3 Pour the mixture into the prepared cake pan and bake for 1¼–1½ hours, or until a toothpick (cocktail stick) inserted in the center of the cake comes out clean. Let cool in the pan.

4 To make the frosting, put the confectioners' sugar, cocoa, and softened butter into a bowl and mix well. Gradually add a little hot water, 1 tbsp at a time, mixing well, until the frosting is of a spreadable consistency. Spread the frosting evenly over the top of the cake and swirl gently with a fork. Sprinkle with chopped nuts, if you like, and, when the frosting has set, cut the gingerbread into 2½in/6cm squares.

Witches' cats and hats

Purrrfect for Halloween or any other witchy-themed occasion. Look for different shapes of cat cutters and edible Halloween sprinkles in green, orange, and black.

1 Preheat the oven to 325°F/160°C/Gas 3, and line two baking sheets with baking parchment. Lightly dust the work surface with flour and roll the Chocolate Gingerbread dough evenly to ⅛in/3 mm thick. Use cat and witches' hat cutters to stamp out shapes. Gather up the trimmings and re-roll, then cut out more shapes. Arrange on the baking sheets. Bake in batches in the center of the oven for 10–12 minutes, or until firm and browned at the edges. Allow to cool completely on the baking sheets before icing.

2 Take out 2 tsp of the Royal Icing and put into a small bowl, cover and set aside. Put 3–4 tbsp of the icing into a small bowl and tint this green using the food coloring paste. Cover and set aside. Tint the remaining icing black.

3 Fill a piping bag with a fine tip (nozzle) with the black icing and pipe a fine line around the edge of each cookie. Allow to dry for at least 10 minutes. Flood (page 134) the insides of the outlines with black icing. Tip the orange and black sprinkles into a saucer, and dip the bottom edge of each hat in the sprinkles. Allow to dry for 20 minutes.

4 Fill another piping bag with a fine tip with the green icing and pipe a green band around each hat and a collar on each cat. Carefully sprinkle orange and green sanding sugar on the hat bands. Pipe each cat a set of white eyes and dot with a little black icing. Let dry completely.

all-purpose (plain) flour, for dusting

1 quantity Chocolate Gingerbread dough (page 141)

Royal Icing (page 132)

green and black food coloring pastes

orange and black sprinkles (hundreds and thousands)

orange and green sanding sugar (sanding sprinkles)

Makes 10–12

Gift tags

These pretty tags look gorgeous attached to gifts for a birthday. They also look special for a wedding as personalized place cards. You don't need cookie cutters—just cut out a gift-tag template from card.

all-purpose (plain) flour, for dusting

1 quantity Chocolate Gingerbread dough (page 141)

1 quantity Royal Icing (page 132)

pink and blue food coloring pastes

short lengths of fine ribbon

Makes 10–12

1 Preheat the oven to 325°F/160°C/Gas 3, and line two baking sheets with baking parchment. Using a piece of card, make a gift-tag shaped template by cutting out a rectangle roughly 5 x 3in/13 x 7.5cm. Snip small triangles off the top two corners of the rectangle to make a tag. Dust the work surface with flour and roll the Chocolate Gingerbread dough evenly to a thickness of ⅛in/3mm. Use the template to cut out shapes. Use the trimmings to cut more shapes.

2 Arrange the cookies on the baking sheets. Using a wooden toothpick (cocktail stick), make a hole in the top of each tag to thread a ribbon through once iced. Bake the gingerbread in batches in the center of the oven for 10–12 minutes, or until firm and browned at the edges. Allow the cookies to cool before icing.

3 Put 3 tbsp of the Royal Icing in a bowl, and transfer half the remaining icing to another bowl. Use the food coloring to tint one of the larger amounts of icing pink and the other blue. Fill a piping bag with a fine tip (nozzle) with the white icing. Pipe outlines (page 133) on each cookie and allow to dry. Flood (page 134) them with pink or blue icing and dry for 20 minutes.

4 Tint the remaining pink and blue icing a darker shade and put into clean piping bags. Pipe lines and dots around each tag, and the initial in the center. Let the icing set, before adding the ribbon.

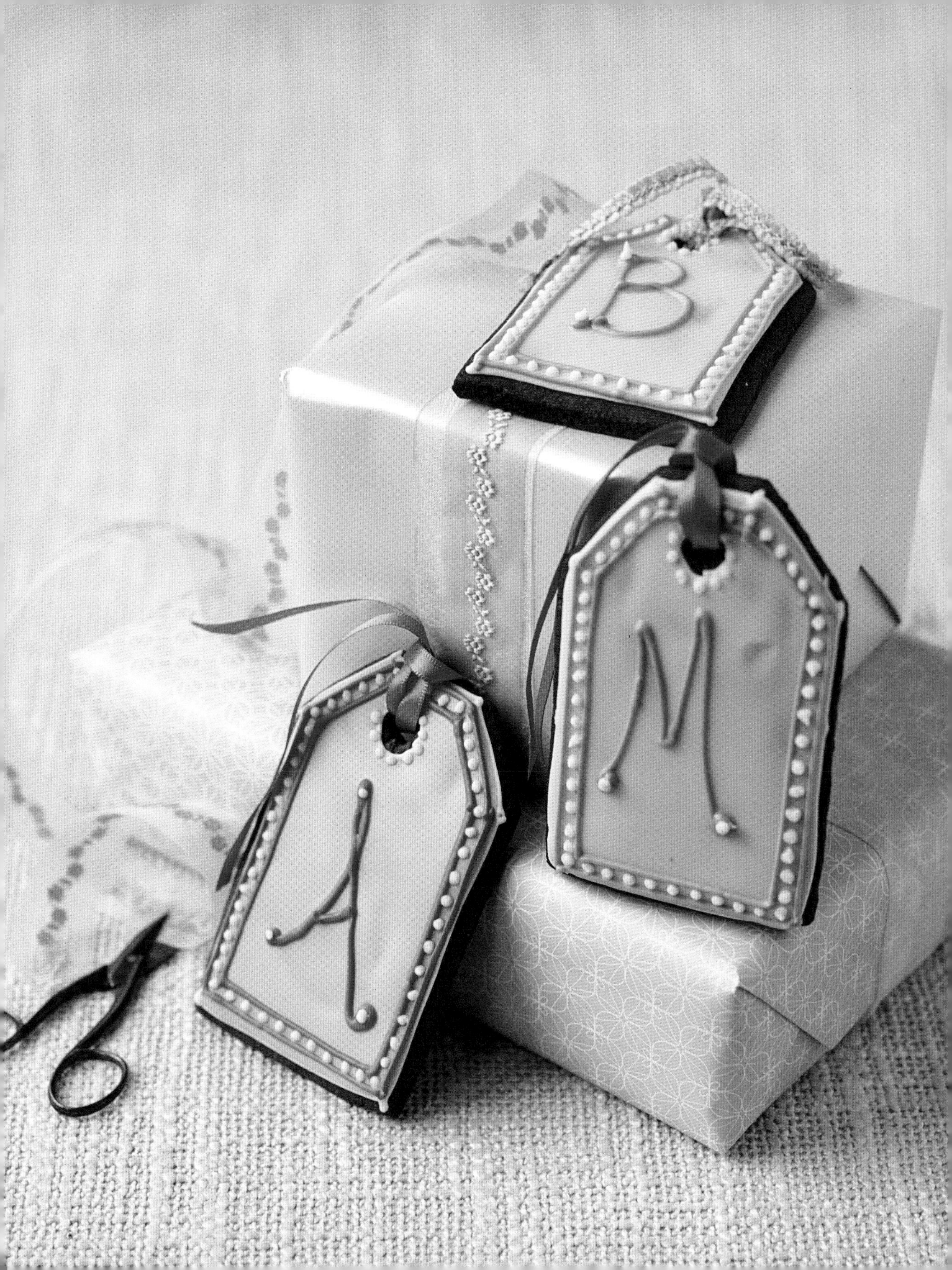
B
M
A

Lebkuchen

In Germany, it wouldn't be Christmas without lebkuchen. This is a lighter version, based on meringue and nuts, and with just six spices, instead of the traditional seven—crisp and light, but densely flavored.

¾ cup/100g almonds (not blanched)

1oz/25g bittersweet (plain) chocolate, coarsely chopped

2 tbsp mixed peel, very finely chopped

½ tsp ground cinnamon

½ tsp ground ginger

¼ tsp freshly grated nutmeg

¼ tsp ground black pepper

¼ tsp ground cloves

¼ tsp ground allspice

2 extra-large (UK large) egg whites

1 cup/115g confectioners' (icing) sugar, sifted

To decorate

5oz/150g good bittersweet (plain) chocolate, coarsely chopped

Makes 16

1 Preheat the oven to 300°F/150°C/Gas 2, and line two baking sheets with baking parchment. Put the almonds and chopped chocolate into the bowl of a food processor and process until the mixture looks like fine crumbs. Mix with the finely chopped peel and all the spices.

2 Put the egg whites into a clean, grease-free bowl and, using an electric whisk, whisk until stiff peaks form. Gradually whisk in the confectioners' sugar, then whisk for another minute to make a very stiff, glossy meringue. Sprinkle the spice mixture over the top and gently fold in with a large metal spoon.

3 Take tablespoonfuls of the mixture and drop them onto the baking sheets, spacing them well apart. Using a round-bladed knife, spread out each mound to a disc about 3in/7.5cm across. Bake for 15–20 minutes, until pale gold and firm.

4 Transfer the lebkuchen to a wire rack and let cool completely. When cold, peel them off the baking parchment. To decorate, put the chocolate in a heatproof bowl set over a pan of gently simmering water, making sure the bowl doesn't touch the water. Stir gently until melted, then remove from the heat. Spread some melted chocolate over one side of each lebkuchen with a metal spatula, then leave on baking parchment to set. Store in an airtight container and eat within four days.

CHAPTER 3

Chocolates *and* Candy

Richly flavored fudge, sugar eggs with a surprise in the center, old-fashioned and delicate chocolate cameos—these are just a few of the chocolates and candies you will find in this chapter. Although store-bought chocolates are always tempting, you really can't beat homemade for flavor and texture, and they say so much more when presented as a gift. When it comes to candymaking, it's a fun way to make a sweet treat into something worth giving. For someone you really care about, make one of the sweet delights from this chapter, gift-wrapped to look extra special.

Violet and rose creams

The subtle flavor of the violet or rose emerges as the chocolate coating melts in your mouth. A traditional Victorian treat, these creams are irresistible and a true indulgence. They are unbelievably easy to make and delightful to receive as a gift. Beware—make lots, or you'll eat them before you've had time to wrap them up!

12oz/350g ready-to-roll fondant (sugar paste)

1 tbsp liquid glucose or
light corn (golden) syrup

½ tbsp violet syrup

purple food coloring for violet creams, pink for rose creams (optional)

½ tbsp rose water

cornstarch (cornflour)

7oz/200g good-quality bittersweet (plain) chocolate, coarsely chopped

small sugar flowers, to decorate

Makes 30

1 Divide the fondant in half. Mix together, in a food processor or by hand, one piece of fondant, ½ tbsp liquid glucose or corn syrup, the violet flavoring, and a little purple food coloring, if using. The mixture should have a loose consistency but be firm enough to handle. Mix the other piece of fondant in the same way, using the rose water and pink coloring.

2 Dust your hands very lightly with cornstarch when handling the mixture. Form about 15 small ovals from each color and leave them to dry overnight on wax paper or baking parchment.

3 Put the chocolate in a heatproof bowl over a pan of gently simmering water, making sure the bowl doesn't touch the water. Heat gently until the chocolate has melted. Remove from the heat and let cool slightly.

4 Dip the creams into the chocolate, then leave to dry on a wire rack. When the chocolates have cooled a little more, add a sugar flower on top. Allow the chocolates to set completely. Store in an airtight container in a cool, dry place for up to one month.

Chocolate-coated toffee balls

These brightly colored balls are such fun. They are hard, so roll them into very small balls so that they are bite-size and don't pull your teeth out when you eat them! They make beautiful gifts if wrapped up in cellophane, or put into glass jars, and tied with a ribbon.

1 Put the cream, sugar, cocoa, honey, and butter into a large pan and melt together over medium heat, stirring continuously until all the sugar has dissolved. Bring to a boil and then simmer until the mixture reaches 240°F/115°C on a candy (sugar) thermometer—the soft ball stage (page 136)—stirring occasionally.

2 Let cool to a comfortable temperature so that you can handle the mixture, but don't allow the mixture to cool so much that it starts to set. Roll pieces of the warm mixture with your fingers to make very small, bite-size balls. Place the balls on a sheet of baking parchment and cool completely.

3 Put the chocolate in a heatproof bowl over a pan of gently simmering water, making sure the bowl doesn't touch the water. Heat gently until the chocolate has completely melted. Remove from the heat.

4 Dip the toffee balls, one by one, into the chocolate, then drop each ball into a small cup and scatter with sprinkles. Swirl the ball around in the cup so that the sprinkles coat it, then place the ball on a sheet of baking parchment to set. Store in an airtight container.

1 cup/250ml heavy (double) cream

1½ cups/300g superfine (caster) sugar

½ cup/55g unsweetened cocoa powder

1 tbsp honey

¼ stick/25g butter

For the coating

4oz/115g good-quality bittersweet (plain) chocolate, coarsely chopped

colored sprinkles (hundreds and thousands)

Makes 20

Turkish delight

An exotic treat traditionally from the Middle East, Turkish delight is said to date back over 200 years and was originally served as a love token. This is a fun and sticky project to make with children.

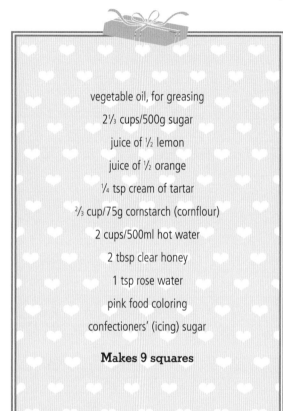

vegetable oil, for greasing

2⅓ cups/500g sugar

juice of ½ lemon

juice of ½ orange

¼ tsp cream of tartar

⅔ cup/75g cornstarch (cornflour)

2 cups/500ml hot water

2 tbsp clear honey

1 tsp rose water

pink food coloring

confectioners' (icing) sugar

Makes 9 squares

1 Lightly grease a shallow 8in/20cm square cake pan (tin) with a little vegetable oil. In a pan, mix together the sugar, ½ cup/125ml water, and the lemon and orange juice. Heat over medium heat, stirring until the sugar has dissolved. Increase the heat and boil without stirring until the mixture reaches 240°F/115°C on a candy (sugar) thermometer—the soft ball stage (page 136). Take the pan off the heat. Gently stir in the cream of tartar, then let cool for 10–15 minutes.

2 Mix ⅓ cup/75ml cold water with the cornstarch in a pitcher (jug). Add the hot water and stir. Pour into a separate pan. Bring to a boil slowly over low heat, stirring continuously until the mixture is thick and smooth. Take off the heat. Carefully pour the hot sugar syrup, a little at a time, into the cornstarch mixture, stirring with a wooden spoon. Put the pan back on the heat and slowly bring to a simmer. Cook gently for 25 minutes stirring occasionally to prevent sticking. Take off the heat.

3 Stir in the honey, rose water, and a few drops of food coloring. Let cool for 2 minutes, then pour into the cake pan. Let cool completely, then put in the refrigerator to set overnight.

4 Sift some confectioners' sugar over the work surface. Run a knife around the edge of the pan, then invert it onto the sugar. Sift more sugar over the Turkish Delight and cut into squares. Store in an airtight container and eat within four days.

Chocolate Easter eggs

Making your own Easter eggs couldn't be easier—just choose the mold of your choice and off you go. Chocolate eggs are simple and economical to make, and they look so pretty and original as gifts.

about 3½oz/100g good-quality bittersweet (plain) or white chocolate, coarsely chopped (the quantity of chocolate will depend on the size of the mold)

Royal Icing (page 132), melted chocolate, sugar flowers, and ribbon, to decorate (optional)

Makes 4

1 Put the chocolate in a heatproof bowl over a pan of gently simmering water, making sure the bowl doesn't touch the water. Heat gently until the chocolate has melted. Remove from the heat and let cool slightly.

2 Clean four small Easter egg molds thoroughly, polishing them with a cotton bud. This makes it easier to turn out the finished eggs. Using a small paintbrush, coat the insides of the molds with a thin layer of chocolate. Chill the molds for about 10 minutes. Repeat by painting another layer of chocolate, then chill for 10 minutes. Repeat until you have three or four layers. Leave the last layer in the mold for 20 minutes. When the chocolate is completely set, gently remove the egg from the mold.

3 Place a nonstick baking sheet in the oven until hot. Remove from the oven and put the edges of the eggs face down on the hot sheet for 2–3 seconds only, so that they melt slightly. Stick the halves together. Chill for 5 minutes.

4 To decorate, handle the eggs as little as possible, or they will melt. Place each egg in a glass so that it can't move around. Using either Royal Icing or melted chocolate, pipe writing or a design onto each egg. Use sugar flowers to decorate further, using a small dot of melted chocolate to stick them in place. Decorate with ribbon, if you like.

Apple jelly candy

Jelly candies are real comfort food and delicious made using apple or any fruit that can be cooked to a thick pulp, such as pears, apricots, or plums. A selection of colors will look like jewels in a gift box.

1 Roughly chop the apples, then put in a pan and cover with just enough water to stop the fruit sticking during cooking. Bring to a boil, then simmer gently until the fruit is very soft. Sieve the pulp to remove any excess liquid or purée in a blender.

2 Weigh the fruit purée and return it to the pan with an equal amount of superfine sugar. Put the pan back on the heat and stir in the lemon juice. Heat gently until the sugar has dissolved, then boil rapidly until the mixture becomes a thick paste. Take the pan off the heat.

3 Dissolve the gelatin in a small amount of warm water according to the pack instructions, and add to the fruit paste, stirring thoroughly to mix. Pour the mixture into a baking pan large enough to hold all the mixture, and let set overnight.

4 Put the sugar for dusting in a bowl. Using a small heart-shaped cutter, cut out the jellies and then roll each one in the sugar until evenly coated. Lay the jellies on a sheet of baking parchment to dry at room temperature. Store in an airtight container, but do not refrigerate.

2¼lb/1kg apples, peeled and cored

superfine (caster) sugar

juice of 1 lemon

2 envelopes (sachets) of gelatin

1 cup/125g granulated sugar, to dust

Makes 20

Christmas truffles

These traditional confections are great for Christmas just as they are, but they can also be decorated with scraps of red and green fondant to look like holly berries and leaves, or with Royal Icing to resemble a traditional round Christmas pudding. You could also add a splash of brandy or rum to the mixture for extra richness.

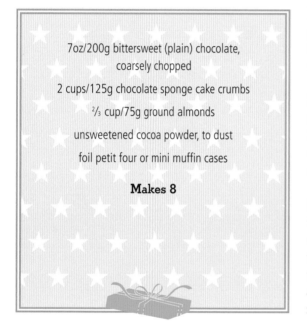

7oz/200g bittersweet (plain) chocolate, coarsely chopped

2 cups/125g chocolate sponge cake crumbs

²/₃ cup/75g ground almonds

unsweetened cocoa powder, to dust

foil petit four or mini muffin cases

Makes 8

1 Put the chocolate in a heatproof bowl over a pan of gently simmering water, making sure the bowl doesn't touch the water. Stir occasionally until melted, then remove the bowl from the heat.

2 Stir in the sponge cake crumbs and ground almonds. When thoroughly combined, cover the bowl and chill for 30 minutes, or until firm. (The mixture can be kept in the refrigerator at this stage, tightly covered, for up to three days.)

3 Using a teaspoon of mixture for each truffle, roll the mixture into neat balls with your hands then drop them into a small bowl of cocoa and shake to coat lightly. Set each truffle in a foil case. Chill until firm, then pack into boxes or store in an airtight container. Store in a cool place or the refrigerator and eat within one week.

Butterscotchies

These are a cross between blondies and brownies, with caramels, chocolate chips, nuts, and caramel frosting. If you can make spun sugar for decoration, all the better.

1 Preheat the oven to 325°F/160°C/Gas 3, and grease and line an 8 x 12in/20 x 30cm baking pan. Tip the pecans onto a baking sheet and lightly toast in the oven for 5 minutes. Chop roughly and let cool.

2 Sift together the flour, baking powder, baking soda, and salt. In a separate bowl, using an electric whisk, cream together the butter and sugars until pale and light. Gradually add the eggs, beating well after each addition. Stir in the vanilla extract. Fold in the flour until well mixed, then stir in the chocolate chips, pecans, and caramels. Spoon the mixture into the baking pan, level the top and bake for 25 minutes, or until just firm to the touch. Cool completely in the pan.

3 To decorate, put the sugar and 1 tbsp water in a small, heavy-based pan over low–medium heat and let the sugar dissolve without stirring. Raise the heat and continue to cook until the sugar turns a deep amber. Remove from the heat and add the cream—the caramel will bubble furiously and harden—but stir to melt it into the cream, then leave until completely cool. Beat the butter until light and fluffy, then add the cold caramel in a steady stream and stir until smooth.

4 Remove the cakes from the pan and cut into squares. Spoon the caramel frosting into a piping bag with a plain tip (nozzle) and pipe a swirl on top of each. Add some spun sugar, if you like.

¾ cup/75g shelled pecans

scant 2 cups/225g all-purpose (plain) flour

1 tsp baking powder

½ tsp baking soda (bicarbonate of soda)

a pinch of salt

1 stick plus 2 tbsp/150g butter, softened

¾ cup/150g light brown (demerara) sugar

½ cup/100g unrefined superfine (golden caster) sugar

2 eggs, lightly beaten

1 tsp vanilla extract

⅓ cup/50g chocolate chips

10 caramel squares

To decorate

¾ cup/150g superfine (caster) sugar

⅔ cup/150ml/ heavy (double) cream

1¾ sticks/200g butter, softened

spun sugar (optional)

Makes 16–20

Chocolate and cream fudge

A quick and easy recipe for one of the most popular types of fudge. Since almost everyone loves fudge, an offering of a few squares of this richly flavored version is sure to please.

½ stick/55g unsalted butter, diced, plus extra for greasing

3½oz/100g bittersweet (plain) chocolate, coarsely chopped

2 tbsp light (single) or whipping cream

1 tsp vanilla extract or dark rum

1 tbsp corn (golden) syrup

2 cups/225g confectioners' (icing) sugar, sifted

Makes about 20

1 Grease a shallow 7in/18cm baking pan. Put the chocolate and butter in a heatproof bowl over a pan of gently simmering water, making sure the bowl doesn't touch the water. Stir frequently until melted, then remove the bowl from the heat and gently stir in the cream, then the vanilla extract or rum, followed by the corn syrup.

2 Using a wooden spoon, and then your hands, work in the confectioners' sugar 1 tbsp at a time, to make a thick, smooth fudge. If the mixture starts to stiffen before all the sugar has been incorporated, return the bowl to the heat for a minute or so.

3 Transfer the mixture to the prepared pan and press in evenly. Chill until firm, then turn out and cut into squares using a large, sharp knife. Store in the refrigerator and eat within ten days.

Candied orange peel

These zingy chocolate-coated slivers of orange peel are very easy to make and look especially pretty when presented in a crisp white gift box. The combination of citrus and chocolate makes a perfect after-dinner treat.

1 Using a sharp knife, cut the oranges into quarters, and remove the flesh and as much of the pith as possible without damaging the peel of the orange. Cut the peel into strips about ½in/1cm wide. Set aside on a chopping board.

2 Put the water and sugar in a pan, bring to a boil, and boil for 5 minutes. Add the orange peel strips and simmer in the sugar and water mixture for about 2 hours—during this time the mixture should reduce significantly. Remove from the heat and let cool. Drain the peel and let cool on baking parchment.

3 Put the chocolate in a heatproof bowl over a pan of gently simmering water, making sure the bowl doesn't touch the water. Melt gently, then stir the chocolate with a wooden spoon. Dip the orange peel strips into the chocolate so that about half their length is covered. Place the strips back on the baking parchment and let cool completely.

4 Tie the chocolate-coated citrus sticks together in bundles of three with short lengths of ribbon tied in a simple knot. Trim the ribbon ends diagonally to prevent them from fraying.

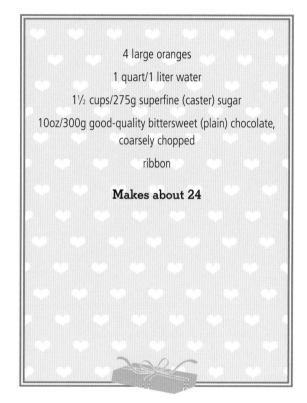

4 large oranges

1 quart/1 liter water

1½ cups/275g superfine (caster) sugar

10oz/300g good-quality bittersweet (plain) chocolate, coarsely chopped

ribbon

Makes about 24

Chocolate cameos

These beautiful chocolate cameos will make a gorgeous, tasty gift. This design is based around the classic profile of a woman in an oval frame, which was popular during the reign of Queen Victoria. The molds are readily available from craft stores and online.

7oz/200g white chocolate, coarsely chopped

10oz/300g milk chocolate, coarsely chopped

pink and blue food coloring pastes

Makes 16 cameos

1 Put the white chocolate in a heatproof bowl over a pan of gently simmering water, making sure the bowl doesn't touch the water. Melt gently, then stir the chocolate with a wooden spoon. Let cool slightly. Take a cameo mold and use a paintbrush to paint the detail of the lady inside the mold using the melted white chocolate, taking care to stay within the correct part of the pattern. Tap the mold gently to settle the chocolate, then chill for 15 minutes until it has set.

2 To make milk chocolate cameos, melt the milk chocolate as above. Spoon the chocolate over the white painted lady to fill the mold to the top. Give the mold a good tap and chill for 30 minutes.

3 To make pink and blue cameos, remove some of the white chocolate from the bowl and add pink or blue coloring, then mix well. If you have a steady hand, you can paint a little colored chocolate detail into the cameo before painting in the white chocolate. Fill the mold with colored chocolate as described for milk chocolate in step 2. Chill each layer as before.

4 Remove the mold from the refrigerator, turn upside down, and gently tap the plastic to remove the chocolate. It will fall out easily.

Crystal sugar eggs

These beautiful rainbow sugar eggs make an amazing Easter display and are a fantastic idea for an edible gift box, too. Choose a candy or a little gift to put inside each egg to surprise your friends! You will need half-egg molds that you buy in two sheets, giving you six complete eggs when the halves are put together.

2 ½ cups/500g superfine (caster) sugar

2 tsp meringue powder or egg white powder

food coloring pastes in assorted colors

6 small candies or treats to fit inside the eggs

Makes 6 eggs

1 Measure out your sugar into four separate bowls containing ½ cup/125g each. Add ½ tsp meringue powder to each bowl, and mix together.

2 Put ½ tsp water into a small bowl. Mix in a little food coloring using a toothpick (cocktail stick).

3 Pour the colored water mix into a bowl of sugar and mix thoroughly with your hands. The sugar will feel like damp sand. You should be able to squeeze the sugar mix and leave an imprint from your hand when it is ready to mold.

4 Repeat steps 2 and 3 using a different color each time until you have prepared four bowls of colored sugar. Make the eggs as overleaf.

5 Using a teaspoon, spoon a little of one color into a small half-egg mold in a sheet of molds. Pack it down tightly using your finger or the spoon.

6 Follow with a second color.

7 then continue with other colors, packing each down as you go to create rainbow-striped layers. You should have at least three to four layers in different colors. Repeat with the other molds in the sheet.

8 Once you have packed each half-egg mold in the sheet to the top, scrape off any excess sugar so that the top of the mold is level. Put a piece of baking parchment onto a baking sheet and invert onto the mold. Hold the baking sheet and the

back of the mold tightly, then flip the mold and baking sheet over.

9 Gently lift off the mold, the eggs should stay in place. Leave the eggs on the baking sheet in a cool, dry place (make sure it is not too humid) for at least 4 hours or overnight.

10 Once the eggs are dry, take each half and smooth any edges with a tsp, then begin to hollow out the eggs: put the tip of your teaspoon into the center of the egg and begin to twist. Continue until the edge of the egg is about ½in/1cm thick. (6) Put a candy or treat inside and attach the two halves. Carefully arrange in an attractive display, or pack into gift boxes.

CHAPTER 4

Preserves, Chutneys, *and* Oils

If you're looking for an alternative to a baked gift for someone you care about, this chapter contains some preserves, chutneys, and oils that are particularly suitable for making as presents. There are fruit conserves that can be used to jazz up ice cream or pancakes, and richly flavored chutneys to serve with Thanksgiving or Christmas meals, or to add a fruity tang to sandwiches, cheeses, or cold meats. And if you're looking for a gift for someone who is happiest when they are in the kitchen cooking something amazing, prepare an attractive bottle filled with best-quality oil, aromatic with herbs or spices.

Strawberry and vanilla jam

Let's face it, strawberry jam is the real classic and a wonderful gift in summer. This fragile berry isn't great for storing, so for the best jam, capture the fruit at its freshest and preserve it in recognizable chunks. This really is summer in a jar, and here strawberries are teamed with vanilla, making the perfect partnership.

1 Split the vanilla bean lengthwise into four pieces and place in a bowl with the strawberries, tucking the bean pieces in among the fruit. Cover with the sugar and leave for 12 hours or overnight.

2 Pour the fruit, vanilla bean, and juice into a preserving pan and add the lemon juice. Cook over low heat until the sugar has dissolved, stirring only occasionally so that the fruit stays intact. Increase the heat and boil rapidly to reach setting point (220°F/105°C; or when a small blob of jam dropped onto a chilled plate sets in a few minutes). Skim if necessary (page 139).

3 Remove the vanilla bean pieces, and scrape out the seeds, then add them to the jam. Discard the beans. Stir the seeds through the jam.

4 Pour the jam into warm, sterilized jars (page 137) and seal (page 139). Store in a cool, dark place for up to nine months.

1 vanilla bean (pod)

2¼lb/1kg strawberries, hulled, and larger fruits halved

3¾ cups/750g jam sugar

juice of 3 small lemons

Makes 3lb/1.3kg

Red fruit conserve

Frozen red fruits are available all year around, and this conserve makes an attractive Christmas gift. This recipe, made with a large bag of raspberries, strawberries, cherries, blueberries, red currants, and black currants, makes a juicy, thick conserve to serve warm or at room temperature with pancakes, ice cream, or muffins.

2¼lb/1kg frozen unsweetened red fruits

1 cup/200g superfine (caster) sugar

1 tbsp lemon juice

1 cup/340g jar red currant jelly

Makes about 1¼ quarts/1.25 liters

1 Put the frozen fruits, sugar, lemon juice, and red currant jelly into a large nonmetallic bowl. Cover and leave for 2–4 hours, or overnight in the refrigerator, until the fruit has thawed.

2 Put the mixture into a large, heavy, non-aluminum pan and bring to a boil. Simmer steadily for 10 minutes, or until the mixture has thickened. Remove the pan from the heat and stir gently.

3 Pour the conserve into warm, sterilized jars (page 137) and seal (page 139). Let cool, then store in the refrigerator and use within two weeks.

Cranberry and basil relish

The perfect gift to take to a Thanksgiving or Christmas dinner. As well as being a traditional and exquisite accompaniment for roast poultry, the relish goes into sandwiches made with cold turkey and ham or simply alongside some strongly flavored cheese.

2 tbsp olive oil

1 red onion, finely chopped

2 garlic cloves, crushed

3 cups/350g fresh or frozen cranberries
(no need to thaw)

½ cup/100g raw cane (demerara) sugar

¼ cup/50ml red wine vinegar

a small bunch of fresh basil, leaves only

¼ tsp coarse sea salt

ground black pepper

Makes 1¾ cups/400ml

1 Heat the olive oil in a large, heavy skillet or sauté pan, preferably nonstick. Add the onion and garlic, and cook gently, stirring occasionally, for 5 minutes.

2 Add the remaining ingredients to the pan and stir well. Cook over medium heat, stirring frequently, until very thick, about 10 minutes. Taste and adjust the seasoning, adding more salt if necessary.

3 Spoon into warm, sterilized jars (page 137) and seal (page 139). Let cool, then store in the refrigerator and use within one month.

Cranberry and raisin chutney

A special homemade gift for Thanksgiving or Christmas, this chutney is colorful and decorative, and goes beautifully with turkey and ham, hot or cold poultry, salads, and cheese. Try making your own labels— they are very easy to create on a computer and lend an extra personal touch to the gift.

1 Put all the ingredients, except the cranberries, into a preserving pan or heavy stainless steel pan. Add ¾ cup/175ml water, bring to a boil, reduce the heat, and simmer until tender.

2 Add the cranberries and simmer for 40 minutes, or until the fruit is soft but not disintegrated.

3 Spoon into warm, sterilized jars (page 137) and seal (page 139). Store in a cool dark place for 2–3 weeks before using. After opening, store in the refrigerator and use within three months.

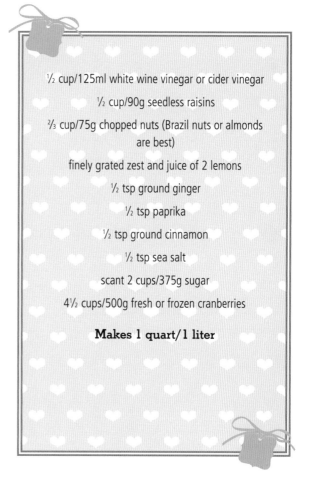

½ cup/125ml white wine vinegar or cider vinegar

½ cup/90g seedless raisins

⅔ cup/75g chopped nuts (Brazil nuts or almonds are best)

finely grated zest and juice of 2 lemons

½ tsp ground ginger

½ tsp paprika

½ tsp ground cinnamon

½ tsp sea salt

scant 2 cups/375g sugar

4½ cups/500g fresh or frozen cranberries

Makes 1 quart/1 liter

Flavored oils

Flavored oils, scented with aromatic spices, chilies, and fresh herbs make a wonderful gift, especially for someone who has a love of cooking. Always use a good-quality oil, preferably extra-virgin olive oil.

Orange and saffron oil

5–7 long thin strips of fresh or dried orange zest

½–1 tsp saffron threads

1 tsp coriander seeds, bruised

a fresh rosemary sprig, about 5in/13cm long

extra-virgin olive oil

Makes about 2 cups/500ml

Put the orange zest, saffron, coriander seeds, and rosemary sprig into a sterilized glass bottle (page 137). Using a funnel, add enough olive oil to fill the bottle (leaving enough room at the top if you are using a cork or stopper.) Seal tightly and store in a cool dark place for two weeks before using.

Chili oil

3 fresh bay leaves

6 fresh small red chiles

1 teaspoon whole black peppercorns

olive oil

Makes 2–2½ cups/ 500–625ml

Put the bay leaves, chilies, and peppercorns into a sterilized glass bottle (page 137). Using a funnel, add enough olive oil to fill the bottle (leaving enough room at the top if you are using a cork or stopper.) Seal tightly and store in a cool dark place for two weeks before using.

Green herb oil

sprig of tarragon

sprig of rosemary

sprig of sage

sprig of thyme

3 small fresh bay leaves

1 teaspoon whole black or red peppercorns

olive oil

Makes 2–2½ cups/ 500–625ml

Push the herbs into a sterilized glass bottle (page 137). Add the peppercorns. Using a funnel, add enough olive oil to fill the bottle (leaving enough room at the top if you are using a cork or stopper.) Seal tightly and store in a cool dark place for one week before using.

Baking and decorating equipment

You can make some of the gifts in this book with the minimum of baking equipment, but for a range of beautiful treats, look out for unusual cookie cutters, coloring pastes, and edible decorations.

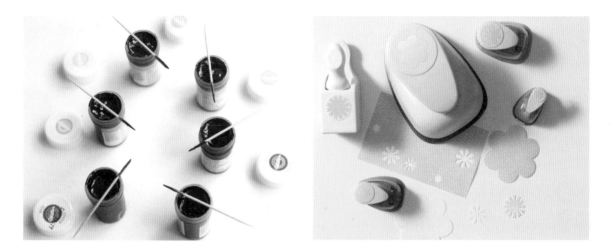

MAKING CANDIES AND DECORATING

Some candies require very few items of equipment for good results. A candy (sugar) thermometer is a useful purchase if you plan to try several of the recipes that involve working with heated sugar, such as the toffees. For the fudge and fondant (sugarpaste)–shaped creams, however, you'll only need basic baking equipment. If you want to make more ornate candy or chocolates, you will need to buy some molds. There is a wide range to choose from, including the elegant cameo molds and the Easter egg molds used in this book. If you plan to work with hard candy (boiled sweets), make sure you choose a mold that is suited to the task.

Food coloring pastes, available in an array of colors, are essential for coloring fondant and icings, and give a far better result than liquid colorings because they don't dilute the icing. Add them gradually using a toothpick (cocktail stick).

Candies, cupcakes, and cookies can be transformed simply by adding edible decorations. Fondant shapes, edible pearls, silver balls, jewels, flowers, and stars can give that eye-catching finishing touch, but also look for edible glitter, silver or gold powder, sanding sugar, or simply sprinkles (hundreds and thousands). Present your candies in dainty, petit four paper cases.

MAKING CAKES

For cake-making, you will need a baking pan (tin), for cakes such as brownies, various cake pans, and perhaps some individual shaped pans. For cupcakes and muffins, you need one or two 12-cup muffin pans, plus the paper cases to line them. Measuring equipment is a must, whether you use measuring cups and spoons or scales. You will also need a fine sieve for sifting flour. A wooden spoon is a basic, but an electric whisk will reduce your preparation time. You will also need a wire rack for cooling your baked cakes.

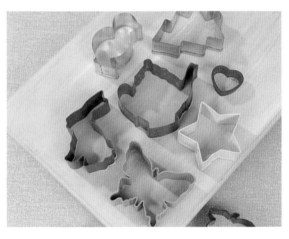

MAKING COOKIES

Basic equipment for making cookies includes a rolling pin, ruler, and flat baking sheets. For cutting out cookie shapes you will need cookie cutters, which are available as rounds—fluted or plain—squares or shaped, such as stars, flowers, animals, people (for gingerbread people), and novelty shapes, such as the Halloween and baby shoes used in this book. You can also make simple paper templates to cut around using a sharp knife (see the Gift Tags on page 88). You will need

baking parchment for lining the baking sheets, and toothpicks (cocktail sticks) for making holes in cookies that will be hung as decorations. Some cookies are piped, using a piping bag or squeezy bottle fitted with a wide fluted tip (nozzle). A wire rack for cooling is essential.

For decorating, you will need piping bags with icing tips in fine, medium, and thick sizes, soft paintbrushes, and edible glue (although you can use a syrup instead—see page 136). A small rolling pin and narrow spacers are also handy. See also the decoration suggestions on the opposite page.

Making and using icing

Royal Icing gives cookies a perfectly smooth and neat finish. Fondant is a versatile icing for cookies, cakes, and for making candies. Follow the hints on coloring and decorating for a professional look.

ROYAL ICING

Store-bought royal icing sugar is convenient to use – simply follow the instructions on the pack. However, it's also very easy to make it yourself from scratch, but be aware that it uses raw egg whites, although you can buy meringue powder, an egg substitute, and follow the directions on the pack.

2 egg whites or 3 tbsp meringue powder
3⅓–4 cups/375–450g confectioners' (icing) sugar, sifted

Beat the egg whites until foamy, using a wire whisk. Gradually add the confectioners' sugar, and whisk until the desired stiffness is reached— for piping, the icing should hold a solid ribbon trail. If you're not using the icing immediately, cover with plastic wrap (clingfilm). To make piped shapes, fit a piping bag with a suitable tip (nozzle) and fill with the Royal Icing. Line a baking sheet with baking parchment and pipe shapes onto the paper. Set aside for at least 24 hours until set solid. Shapes will keep for up to one week in an airtight container. Store the shapes between layers of baking parchment.

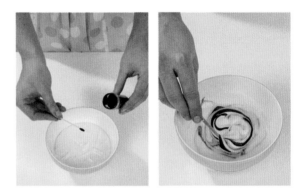

TINTING ROYAL ICING

Use either a wooden skewer or toothpick (cocktail stick) to add tiny amounts of food coloring paste to the Royal Icing. (1) Mix thoroughly before adding more coloring. (2) Remember that some colors can intensify over time, so always add the coloring in very small amounts.

MAKING PIPING ICING FOR OUTLINING

Piping icing for an outline should be firm enough to hold its own shape but still soft enough to pipe. For the best results, your equipment must be clean and grease-free. Beat your icing for 5–10 minutes using an electric whisk until it reaches the consistency of a stiff meringue and turns glossy.

Cover it with plastic wrap (clingfilm), making sure it touches the surface of the icing to prevent it from forming a skin. Your icing will be at its best the day that it is made, but it can be kept in the refrigerator for a couple of days. Color it just before you use it.

OUTLINING A COOKIE

When piping icing, make sure the top of the piping bag is tightly folded down so that the bag is taut. squeeze the bag from the top, not the middle, using your dominant hand. You may want to use the fingers of your other hand to steady the bag. The purpose of piping an outline is to create a barrier to hold icing on a cookie, known as "flooding." With your first few projects, you may want to use a wider tip (nozzle) to make a thicker barrier so that the icing is less likely to overflow. As you become more confident, you will be able use a narrow tip, which gives a more subtle outline. You will need one-third of the quantity of icing to outline the cookies and the rest to flood them.

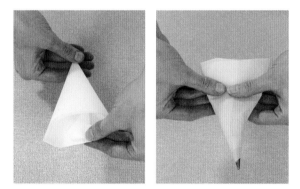

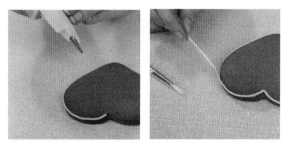

1 Use a piping bag with a tip (nozzle) or make a cone with baking parchment and fold over the top to secure. Then drop a piping tip inside. When ready to pipe the icing, spoon the icing into the bag. Close the bag together using your fingers.

2 Work the icing down the bag with your fingers and fold down the top to close it. When taking a break from icing, store your piping bag in a glass with some damp paper towel in the bottom to stop it from drying out.

1 When outlining the cookie, pipe as close to the edge as possible. Hold the bag at a 45-degree angle, apply even pressure, and move the bag steadily along the cookie. For best results, lift the piping bag tip off the cookie and allow the icing to fall, rather than dragging the tip along the surface of the cookie.

2 If it goes wrong, you can move it with a toothpick (cocktail stick) or use a damp paintbrush to tidy it up. Although the neater the better, don't worry if your outline is not perfect, provided there are no gaps. Leave the outline to dry for a few minutes before flooding the cookie (see overleaf).

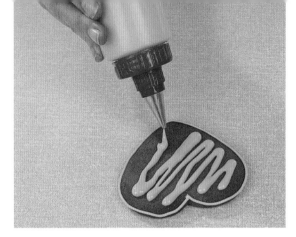

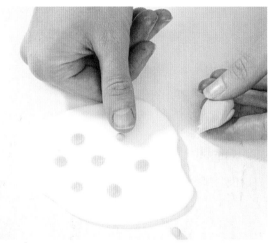

MAKING ICING
FOR FLOODING

To flood your cookies, thin the Royal Icing with
a little water until it reaches the consistency of
emulsion paint. It should be thin enough to spread
when it goes onto the cookie but not so thin that it
runs off the edge. When you start out, it is best to
err on the thicker side, as it is less likely to
overflow.

The exact amount of water you need to add
will depend on the day, the temperature of
your kitchen, the weather, and so on, so add it
teaspoon by teaspoon until you reach the correct
consistency. Once you have iced a few cookies,
you will know what to aim for. Squeeze some icing
onto the cookie, keeping it away from the edges.
You want to squeeze enough icing so that it looks
generously covered, but not so much that it
overflows. Use a toothpick (cocktail stick) to guide
the icing so that it floods any gaps. Leave to dry
completely, before adding further decoration.

POLKA-DOT ICING

To make polka-dot icing, roll out some white icing
as normal. Then roll some small balls of colored
icing between your fingers and squash these down
onto the white icing using your thumb. When all
the balls are in place, gently roll over the icing to
incorporate the dots.

Wet-on-wet technique

To add polka dots to a flooded cookie (see top
right), make up some flooding (or "wet") icing in
another color and put into a piping bag with a
small tip (nozzle). While the cookie is still wet, dot
spots of wet icing onto the flooded icing.

COVERING WITH READY-TO-ROLL FONDANT

Ready-to-roll fondant (sugarpaste), which is also sold as rolled, roll out, or rolled icing, is available in most cake decorating and craft stores, and many supermarkets. It provides a very quick and easy way to decorate cookies and cakes, and for making candies. A moist fondant may stick to a cookie easily, otherwise, to stick the fondant to the cake or cookie, use edible glue or use a little corn (golden) syrup or sugar syrup made from dissolving sugar and warm water in a 1:1 ratio, then brush over the surface.

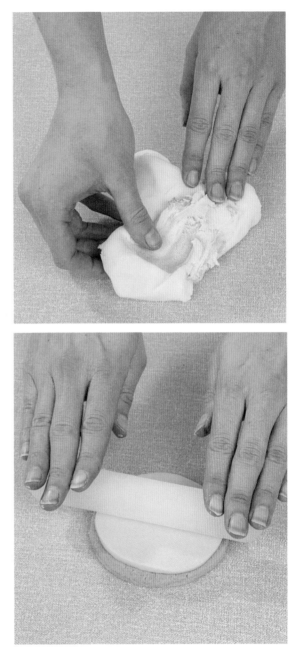

1 Work the fondant between your fingers until it is pliable. Try not to use your palms, as they will make the icing sticky. To color the icing, add tiny amounts of food coloring paste on a toothpick (cocktail stick) and add to the fondant, then knead the fondant until the color is fully blended with no streaks.

2 Roll the fondant out on a work surface dusted with confectioners' (icing) sugar to ⅛in/3mm thick, then cut out with the cookie cutter. If the icing is not too dry, it will stick to the cookie; alternatively, brush the cookie with edible glue or syrup, as above, using a damp brush.

3 Attach the icing to the cookie. If the cookie has spread a little in the oven, lightly roll over the icing to stretch it right to the edges of the cookie. Run your finger around the edge of the icing to smooth it onto the cookie for a perfect finish.

Candy sugar stages

There are five stages in syrup-making. You can test using a candy (sugar) thermometer or by dropping a little of the syrup into cold water. You can also test for setting point when making preserves.

Thread stage, temperature: 230°F /110°C; in cold water the syrup forms a fine, soft thread.

Soft-ball stage, temperature: 240°F/115°C; in cold water the syrup forms a soft ball that you can easily squash between finger and thumb.

Hard-ball stage, temperature: 250°F/120°C; in cold water the syrup forms a firmer, but still pliable ball.

Soft-crack stage, temperature: 270°F/130°C; in cold water the syrup forms thick threads that bend a little, but then break up.

Hard-crack stage, temperature: 300°F/150°C; in cold water the syrup forms thick, brittle threads that break immediately when you bend them.

When making preserves, boil the syrup until setting point is reached:

Setting point, temperature: 220°F/105°C, or when a small blob of preserves, dropped onto a chilled plate sets in a few minutes.

Preserving techniques and equipment

Making preserves is a satisfying hobby, and homemade jams and chutneys are always so much tastier than store-bought. You need to follow some basics to be sure of good results and long storage.

The principle underlying preserving is to prevent the growth of yeasts, molds, and bacteria, which are destroyed when heated to high temperatures to sterilize them. Preserves must then be kept sealed so that air cannot enter. Preserves that are at least 60 per cent sugar are less susceptible to the growth of yeasts, so jams containing less sugar need to be eaten more quickly.

The jars

Use preserving jars, such as mason canning jars in the US or European-style preserving jars, which have glass tops secured by a thick wire clamp. You can also use recycled jam or condiment jars. Make sure that the jars have no chips or cracks and that the lids fit securely. Corrosive materials, such as metal lids, must not come into contact with the preserves, especially if it contains vinegar (as used in chutneys and pickles). The jars must be sterilized before use. Wash the jars in hot soapy water, rinse in hot water, then leave to air-dry. Place a folded dish (tea) towel on an oven shelf and lay the jars on their sides on top. Shortly before you need to use them, heat the oven to 225°F/110°C/ Gas Mark ¼, and leave the jars for 30 minutes. They should still be hot when you fill them with the hot preserve.

Other special equipment

There are a few items that you can buy if you will be doing a lot of preserving:

Preserving pan A non-corrosive, non-reactive preserving pan, large enough to hold large quantities of boiling jam is perfect if you want to make preserves regularly, and is more suitable for preserve making than a large saucepan. A preserving pan is wide and shallow to encourage rapid evaporation when bringing jam to setting point. A good-quality pan will have a thick, heavy base, which will prevent any preserve from burning. Stainless steel is best, and it is certainly necessary when making preserves that contain vinegar. When jam is brought to a rolling boil, it rises up in the pan, so never overfill the pan. If the pan is too small and overfilled, you will either have an overflowing mess of boiling syrupy jam, or in order to prevent this happening, you won't be able to raise the temperature high enough to reach setting point (see page 136).

Long-handled wooden spoon It is essential to keep your hands well away from the boiling syrup, so make sure that the spoon you use is heatproof and has a long handle.

Jar funnel This is essential for pouring hot jam safely into jars. Choose a metal one small enough to fit into most of your jars but wide enough not to become clogged with pieces of fruit. Sterilize and warm the funnel in the oven with the jars. A sterilized, warmed scoop is useful for ladling jam into the funnel.

Jar lifter Special tongs, called a jar lifter, are used for handling the hot jars, but you can use some oven gloves instead.

Jam thermometer Although not essential, this is useful for testing for setting point. Choose one that

goes up to at least 230°F/110°C and has a clip to attach it to the side of the pan.

Sundry equipment If you are tempted by the recipes in this book, you may be interested in making more preserves and may then need some other equipment. Cheesecloth (muslin) for example, is used for holding peel, fruit pits (stones), and spices that require cooking with jams and chutneys. Ready-made jelly bags are used to strain the juices from cooked fruit.

Skimming and sealing

Perfect jams needs to be clear in appearance, and all preserves need to be carefully potted and sealed to ensure that they will store well.

Skimming   During boiling, a scum sometimes forms on jam or jellies caused by bubbles rising to the surface. The scum is harmless, but can spoil the appearance of the preserves. Stir in a small knob of butter to help disperse the scum or use a metal spoon to scoop it away.

Sealing   Once poured into jars, hot jam should be sealed. With mason canning jars or preserving jars, the seal forms part of the lid, but jars with ordinary lids require extra treatment. In the US, a layer of paraffin wax is added—readily available from canning suppliers. Be sure to follow the manufacturer's instructions for melting and pouring the paraffin. In the UK, use waxed disks especially for preserving. Cover your preserves with a lid, or use preserving disks of clear plastic secured with rubber bands. A simple circle of fabric tied with ribbon will make your home-made preserve into an attractive gift.

Labels   Label all your preserves so that you know how long they have been stored. Chutneys and pickles, which benefit from a maturing period, also need to be labeled with this information.

GIFT WRAPPING IDEAS

The recipes in this book are ideal as sweet treats to make as gifts for friends and family. Here are a few presentation ideas to help make your creations look extra special and even more delicious!

As well as recycling containers for your treats, look out for unusual ribbons and pretty papers or containers when shopping. Stationery departments in stores often sell attractively decorated boxes.

A clear cellophane bag finished with a pretty ribbon bow is the easiest way to present cookies and candies—it is simple yet very effective.

Take boxes that once contained necklaces, rings, and watches, and give them a new lease of life by filling them with your own jewelry-inspired creations.

Keep hold of any gift boxes you may have received in the past —these are great to re-use and fill up with cookies and candy.

For that retro candy-store feel, paper bags with simple, bold graphic designs are perfect.

Simple rectangular boxes can be transformed when filled with some colored tissue paper and tied with a ribbon. Fruit cartons in natural materials can add a country touch to treats.

Organza bags are readily available in gift shops in a variety of different sizes, and are ideal to hold elegant candies.

CHOCOLATE GINGERBREAD RECIPE

For use in the recipes on pages 87 and 88.

2 tbsp corn (golden) syrup
2 tbsp molasses (black treacle)
1 extra large (UK large) egg yolk
1⅔ cups/200g all-purpose (plain) flour, plus
    extra for dusting
1 tsp baking powder
3 tbsp unsweetened cocoa powder
2 tsp ground ginger
½ tsp ground cinnamon
¼ tsp freshly grated nutmeg
a pinch of salt
5 tbsp/75g unsalted butter, chilled and diced
⅓ cup packed/75g soft dark brown sugar
½ cup/50g ground almonds

1 Beat together the corn syrup, molasses, and egg yolk in a small bowl.

2 Sift the flour, baking powder, cocoa, spices, and salt into a food processor and add the butter. Pulse until there are no lumps of butter, then add the sugar and almonds, and pulse again. (Alternatively, rub the butter into the flour mixture using your fingers or a pastry cutter, then stir in the sugar and almonds.) With the motor running, add the egg yolk mixture and pulse to bring the mixture together (or stir the egg mixture into the flour mixture).

3 Turn the mixture onto a very lightly floured surface and knead gently to bring together into a smooth ball. Flatten the dough into a disk, wrap in plastic wrap (clingfilm) and chill for 1–2 hours. Use as directed in the recipe.

INDEX

RECIPE CREDITS

Susannah Blake
Christening cupcakes
Halloween cupcakes
Raspberry and lemon Napoleons
Raspberry loveheart cakes
Starry Christmas cupcakes
Wedding cupcakes
White chocolate and lemon truffle balls

Chloe Coker
Baby shoes
Fancy hats
Polka-dot presents

Linda Collister
Cheese palmiers
Chocolate and cream fudge
Chocolate chip biscotti
Christmas mini muffins
Christmas truffles
Cider fruit squares
Cranberry and basil relish
French chocolate fingers
Gingerbread mini muffins
Gingerbread shapes
Lebkuchen
Red fruit conserve
Swedish pepper cookies

Kay Fairfax
Chilli oil
Chocolate gingerbread
Cranberry and raisin chutney
Green herb oil
Orange and saffron oil

Liz Franklin
White chocolate and raspberry tartlets

Gloria Nicol
Strawberry & vanilla jam

Annie Rigg
Advent cupcakes
Butterfly cupcakes
Butterscotchies
Candied clementine with pistachios
Caramel surprise
Christmas trees
Gift tags
Jack-o'-lanterns
Love hearts
Meringue mountain
Mint chocolate kisses
Red velvet Valentine's cupcakes
Witches' cats & hats

Laura Tabor
Chocolate cameos
Crystal cupcakes
Crystal sugar eggs

Nicki Trench
Apple jelly candy
Chocolate-coated toffee balls
Chocolate Easter eggs
Mini florentines
Mini gingerbread men
Turkish delight
Violet and rose Creams

Catherine Woram
Candied orange peel
Valentine cookies

PICTURE CREDITS

Martin Brigdale
Pages 4 top left, 4 top right, 7 top right, 21, 35, 38, 45, 47, 48, 53, 85, 126, 129

Laura Edwards
Pages 2 bottom right, 12, 15, 106

Tara Fisher
Pages 86, 89

Winfried Heinze
Pages 2 top right, 5 top centre, 5 top right, 60, 78, 95, 96, 99, 101, 102

Sandra Lane
Pages 8, 51

Lisa Linder
Page 55

Emma Mitchell
Pages 58, 83, 111

Gloria Nicol
Page 120

Martin Norris
Pages 4 top left, 4 top centre, 69, 70, 71, 73, 81

William Reavell
Pages 2 top left, 5 top left, 7 bottom left, 10, 18, 31, 57, 63, 67, 74, 77, 90, 105, 108, 118, 123, 125

Stuart West
Pages 22, 92, 113, 115, 116, 117

Kate Whitaker
Pages 2 bottom left, 7 bottom right, 17, 25, 26, 27, 28, 32, 37, 41, 42, 43, 65